the springboard God used for her to pen this book and tell the world that God is the real C.E.O. *The Walk at Work* rejuvenates and aligns our beliefs and values so that we can fulfill our ultimate purpose and destiny on the job. A pure delight—it was like eating morsels of fine chocolate."

> —PAMELA PERRY, president and founder of American
> Christian Writers Detroit, newspaper columnist with
> the *Michigan Chronicle* and *Michigan Front Page,* and
> freelance magazine writer

"Andria Hall, child of the manse, has written an ennobling and greatly enriching testimony to her own faith in *The Walk at Work.* These spiritual reflections should inspire all whose vocation is in the marketplace, as well as many others."

> —GARDNER TAYLOR, D.D., pastor emeritus of The
> Concord Baptist Church of Christ

"This is a book that will walk with me everywhere, just like the Jesus I meet in every page of it. I love the Andria I see on TV, and now I feel like I know her better through our mutual Friend."

> —BARBARA CAWTHORN CRAFTON, best-selling author

"What a clever way to mix business with pleasure by showing us that it is okay to bring the Word of God out of the pulpit and into the workplace. Andria explains how to reach out to the Lord, know ourselves better, accept our faults, and see the good in others. The tools she provides will help us fight the devil in ourselves and in those who seek to lead us down the path of anger, bitterness, frustration, and self-doubt. This book is clever, insightful, educational, and uplifting. We can walk at work with our heads held high if we let Christ live in our hearts 24/7."

> —JANICE HUFF, meteorologist, NBC's *Weekend Today*

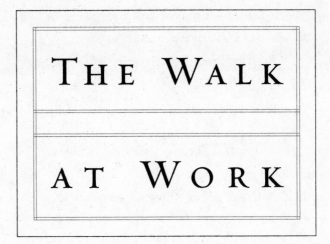

THE WALK

AT WORK

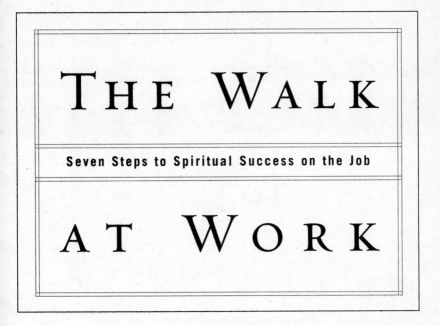

THE WALK

Seven Steps to Spiritual Success on the Job

AT WORK

ANDRIA HALL

WATERBROOK
PRESS

THE WALK AT WORK

PUBLISHED BY WATERBROOK PRESS

2375 Telstar Drive, Suite 160

Colorado Springs, CO 80920

A division of Random House, Inc.

For the purposes of esteeming God to the highest and demeaning the enemy to the lowest, the author
has chosen not to capitalize the name satan or any of his related names.

God made my eyes that I might see.
God made my ears that I might hear.
God made my lips that I might speak.
God made my mind that I might think, and
God made my legs that I might walk.

In all I see, hear, speak, and think, may I walk daily to serve You.

~

For we are His workmanship,
created in Christ Jesus for good works,
which God prepared beforehand
that we should walk in them.

—EPHESIANS 2:10

Contents

Acknowledgments

To God, who *is* Glory, it is only through You, by You, and for You that I am able to dedicate this work to Your Son, my Lord and Savior, Jesus Christ. What a journey!

To my husband, Clayton; my children, Amber, Cameron, and Chase; my family and my friends—your love and support have carried me through.

To my spiritual teachers in Christ, without you shining the Light, I would still be groping to find my way in the dark. Sister Marsha Allen and the rest of the team at The Global Church, Pastor Moussa Toure of Bethel World Outreach Ministries, Pastor Kerwin B. Lee of Berean Christian Church, and Pastor Kevin Brennan of Evangel Church, your knowledge of the Truth continues to feed me the pure milk of the Word of God (see 1 Peter 2:2).

To my editor, Erin Healy, and my new literary family at WaterBrook Press, thank God for your yes. "As the deer pants for the water brooks," just as you all do, so too does my soul thirst after God (see Psalm 42:1).

How to Use This Book

This book is designed primarily to be your guide through a seven-month process of attaining spiritual growth and maturity in your workplace. This is not a book to speed-read through. Think of it instead as a seven-course meal to be savored—one that will feed your soul daily.

Each chapter provides one month's worth of inspirational and motivational readings: The chapters define and explore in detail the seven S.U.C.C.E.S.S. steps. Each discussion is followed by a series of action points, journal exercises, and a prayer that you can apply in day-to-day situations over the course of the month.

The twenty devotional entries that follow each S.U.C.C.E.S.S. step provide readings for four five-day workweeks. These devotionals are written in the first person to help you more easily personalize the principles they offer. Some can be read as prayers. Action points at the end of each will give you an opportunity to begin the process of applying an idea presented in the devotional.

The devotionals are topical, and each keyword is indexed at the back of the book. In addition to using this guide as an organized study, you can also refer to it as needed for wisdom and encouragement when you face specific on-the-job trials, circumstances, and events that affect your Christian walk. It is my belief that when biblical principles permeate the workplace, true success can be achieved.

If You're Still Not Sure

I'm asking you to trust. It's not so much that I'm trying to tell you what to do, but since you did open this book—and I'm the one writing it—I first want to share with you a little secret that, when applied, is guaranteed to yield results. My spiritual mentor, Sister Marsha Allen, has drilled this into my head: "God said it; that settles it!"

For years I believed in God's ability to bless me, but I never gave a second thought to God's unchanging character and, therefore, His need to remain true to Himself. I knew certain activities, while acceptable in our society, were considered sin by God. But I figured He would understand. Well, God does understand our weaknesses, whether sex, drugs, or rock and roll. (Okay, not rock and roll, but the flow doesn't work without it!) God's character, however, while one of love, is also one of righteousness. He is as sure to pour out His judgment as His blessings. That means if we do something, He must respond. This arrangement is great if you are in right standing with Him; it's not so great if you're doing the kinds of things that go against His Word and who He is.

We go down roads that we know we should not be on, get into trouble time and time again, yet wonder, *Why is this happening to me?* Well, stuff happens! Good and bad. But if we want to receive the Lord's mercy rather than His righteous judgment, then we must take spiritual and moral responsibility for all of our thoughts, words, and deeds.

Once I finally got this concept (and believe me, it took so long), accepting God at His Word has made all the difference in my life. His Word simplifies even the smallest of decisions and settles the tiniest of issues. If only we would seek God's opinion about everything, we would know the mind of Christ and then know what to do in all circumstances (see 1 Corinthians 2:16).

But nooooo! We think *we're* equipped to make the choices, don't we? If that's what you think, just remember: When Moses set out to free the Israelites from Pharaoh's clammy clutches, *he* sought God's direction. *They,* however, did not. As a result, what should have been an eleven-day journey ended up taking forty years (see Exodus 16:35)!

Personally, I prefer the eleven-day plan. I really get tired of walking in circles, seeing the same old scenery. You know what I mean? You go through something, you think you've learned your lesson, then up pops the same kind of situation, and you wonder, *Haven't I seen this tree before? Wait a minute! Haven't I been around this track before?* That's what happens when we live life *our* way.

Life is not meant to be some kind of celestial aptitude test that we have to take over and over again. Our heavenly Father wants us to pass. So rather than winging it, why not study the Book written by the One who designed the course? The Holy Bible is the Word of God, which allows believers the awesome advantage of knowing how to live victoriously, at work and anywhere else our Christian walk may take us. Think of it as a cheat sheet with all the answers, one we are allowed to look at as we go through the tests of life.

But you may be thinking, *Well, the Bible was written by men, after all, who lived in a different day* or *Well, back then men had their own agenda. They didn't want women to be liberated and have any fun* or *Come on, those are just fables with lessons attached.* If I'm reading your mind, consider what the sovereign God of the universe says: "All Scripture is given by inspiration of God, and is profitable for doctrine, for reproof, for correction, for instruction in righteousness, that the man of God may be complete, thoroughly equipped for every good work" (2 Timothy 3:16-17).

You do know what BIBLE stands for, right?

Basic

Instructions

Before

Leaving

Earth

Yes, the book you now hold in your hands covers a broad scope of worries in the workplace. Yes, it is a book about changing the definition of success and climbing the corporate ladder *fruitfully* (an idea that I'll explain later). And, yes, it is a seven-month interactive guide, a daily devotional, and a spiritual how-to. But more important than any of that, it is a personal challenge to my readers who don't yet have a personal relationship with Jesus Christ.

We are each aware of life's devastating downfalls and personal defeats. Despite all our efforts at times to overcome, we are often left aching and alone. Jesus is the Ultimate Overcomer, and He is waiting and willing for us to authentically come to Him. We need only to acknowledge our faulty human condition and realize we can be resurrected only by the One who died and rose again. So I hope above all things that each of you will accept Him "for real" and unconditionally as your Lord and Savior. The very God who daily gives you breath wants you to open your heart enough to let Him into your world *and* your work. He is the One, the only One, who can pave your way to effective living at the office.

So if you are tired of constant defeat, if you are worn down and weary, if your only certainty is that the workplace is more uncertain than ever before, I ask you to accept this invitation and pray the following prayer from the bottom of your heart. If you're not ready yet, please do me this one favor: With an earnest and sincere heart, ask God to use this book to make Himself real to you. Read the whole thing and then come back to this section. In the meantime, I pray He will prepare you to receive Him and the multitude of blessings He wants to pour into your life.

Dear Lord Jesus,

I believe that You are alive and are the Son of God. I believe the words that You left for me—a love letter called the Holy Bible— teach the truth that You died for me. I am a sinner saved by Your grace. You conquered death for me. And it will be Your very breath that conquers all my issues in life and at work.

I want to receive Your free gift of eternal salvation. By faith I humbly accept this invitation. Teach me through Your Holy Spirit how to change so that what I say, do, and think is lined up with the Truth of who You are. Show me how to triumph daily at the office by putting You first in every decision that I make. I dedicate my life and my work to You from this day forward. Through faith and prayer, I am an overcomer because of the power in Jesus' name.

Amen.

Seven Steps to Spiritual Success

The foundation of the temple of the LORD was laid in the fourth year, in the month of Ziv. In the eleventh year in the month of Bul, the eighth month, the temple was finished in all its details according to its specifications. He had spent seven years building it.

1 KINGS 6:37-38, NIV

I n 1996 my life in the Lord changed drastically. I'd like to say it was completely by my choice, but sometimes God leaves you *no* choice. That year I came together with my friend Linnie Frank to write a book about God. I'll tell you a little more about that later, but suffice it to say, you can't hide from God. He sees it all. He knows it all. And guess what? He wants it all!

At first His voice came to me as a quiet, gnawing whisper, which got louder the more I surrendered to His call. The more He pressed me into obedience, the more I tried to negotiate. But He would have nothing less than His way with me. The ensuing ups and downs, bumpy roads, and hair-raising turns ultimately allowed me to move closer and closer to God while moving farther and farther away from myself. It has taken me seven years to finally come to the understanding that, because He is faithful, I must be faithful too.

In the midst of my journey through personal change—on September 11, 2001—the world changed too. All of us continue to live daily through the effects of that change. When the World Trade Center crumbled, so did our sense of security and the confidence of the American work force. The wickedness of this terrorist attack in New York City and Washington struck at the heart of America's definition of *freedom.* The days are long over when we could live in routine comfort and head off to work believing the day would hold *business as usual.* However, I believe that through God's gracious Spirit, this horrific act, intended to kill the body, has instead awakened America's corporate soul. It has renewed our spirits' search for God even at the office. Along with the prayers of this nation's saints, I believe 9/11 is bringing revival to our land.

The book of Ezekiel chronicles a time when God's people turned away from Him. It also reveals how crucial it is for God's people to turn back to Him. Perhaps it is human nature that in times of great loss and suffering we are moved, just as in the prophet Ezekiel's time, to take stock of where we are and examine how we can bring God back into our everyday lives.

This book is designed to help you truly understand the meaning of *freedom*—the kind that simply can't be taken away—even by an airplane-turned-missile. The freedom I'm talking about is freedom of the soul. It is in God and God alone that we find true freedom, for "where the Spirit of the Lord is, there is liberty" (2 Corinthians 3:17). This book will equip you to daily walk in that liberty while openly singing a blessed and victorious song of Christian independence.

It is my hope that *The Walk at Work: Seven Steps to Spiritual Success on the Job* will be a helpful tool in conducting the self-examination necessary for you to find "soul satisfaction" in the workplace. Soul satisfaction means consciously living in a contented state of mind and spirit. Soul satisfaction means knowing that wherever we are, we are there because we have been divinely placed there—even if it's smack dab in the middle of a challenge or crisis. Soul satisfaction allows us to daily persevere and endure with peace and joy (see James 1:2-4).

Soul satisfaction is a key indicator of spiritual success, which is not the same as worldly success. In this world, success is often measured *quantitatively:* How much have you accomplished? How much wealth have you amassed? How many rungs of the corporate ladder have you climbed? In this book about spiritual success, I will be focusing on the *qualitative* nature of life in Christ: Have you experienced freedom of your soul? Do you have peace of mind and spirit even in crisis? Do you boldly shine Christ's light into the dark places of your world? Are you going about your Father's business?

When the answer to these questions is yes, our spiritual success is assured. And that success will be made secure not because of what we have accomplished as the result of our own efforts—another trait of worldly success—but because of the great work *Christ* is able to accomplish within us. Our job is to surrender to Him so He can have His way with our lives.

In any given week, many of us spend more time in the office than we do at home. Our work in large part has become our world. But the office can be a dark place. Security concerns, corporate cutbacks, competition, corruption, pressure, and politics make our work environment dim. As believers, however, we are sent by Christ into the world to be a light to those around us. "Let your light so shine before men, that they may see your good works and glorify your Father in heaven" (Matthew 5:16).

Exactly how, though, are we to integrate our Christian walk with our work? The issue of how to publicly express our faith will continue to challenge us daily, but think about this: Jesus Christ Himself had a very public ministry. In addition, while our personal relationship with Him includes the disciplines of private devotions, prayer, and Bible study, these individual acts won't directly accomplish the Lord's desire for us to be "the light of the world" (Matthew 5:14). Private acts of faith should take us to a place where we are quiet, comfortable, and complete in God, yet He calls His children to more. Christ prayed for us: "Sanctify them by Your truth. Your word is truth. As You sent Me into the world, I also have sent them into the world" (John 17:17-18).

Acts 1:8 tells us, "You shall receive power when the Holy Spirit has come upon you; and you shall be witnesses to Me in Jerusalem, and in all Judea and Samaria, and to the end of the earth." When Jesus spoke these words to His disciples, He was also speaking to us. God has christened each one of us to be witnesses of Him first in our homes (Jerusalem), then in our communities (Judea), and then at our places of work (Samaria).

If you look at a map of this region as it was when Christ walked the earth, you will see that Jerusalem is our starting point, since it represents home, the heart of Israelite life. Next, Judea was just a little more than ten miles away. Many people lived in this rural area rather than in the city of Jerusalem. By virtue of its close proximity to Jerusalem, Judea was like an extended community. Samaria, on the other hand, was about thirty-five miles away from Jerusalem. It was a large Palestinian city, a bustling workplace where outsiders called Gentiles lived. This is where the apostles Paul, Philip, and Barnabas preached the gospel and taught many non-Jews about the saving grace of Jesus Christ.

Today, our "Samaria"—our places of employment—is teaming with modern-day Gentiles, people who have never heard the hope and truth of salvation. Our assignment is to spread the message of the gospel, which simply translated means "good news." For us to be most effective, we should pray for the power of the Holy Spirit daily and follow God's direction. We can be spiritually successful at home, in our communities, and yes, even at work, as we represent Christ with a holy lifestyle, spirit-filled work ethics, and daily habits that encourage others and ourselves to keep on walking for Jesus.

In this book, I will encourage you to invite God to take your hand as you attempt to joyfully and purposefully labor for Him. "Be diligent to present yourself approved to God, a worker who does not need to be ashamed, rightly dividing the word of truth" (2 Timothy 2:15). Practicing such diligence in our work requires patience. Just as no building has ever been erected overnight, no believer—himself the very temple of the living God—can expect to remain upright before a Holy Lord without first going through a painful spiritual process. And make no mistake, there is a process, one in which we have no choice but to yield to Him, because He doesn't have to yield—He's God! "Then the word of the LORD came to Solomon, saying: 'Concerning this temple which you are building, if you walk in My statutes, execute My judgments, keep all My commandments, and walk in them, then I will perform My word with you, which I spoke to your father David'" (1 Kings 6:11-12).

Over the past seven years, God has revealed to me the following process of attaining spiritual success in the workplace. Each of the seven steps will take you closer to that place of "present[ing] yourself approved to God" so that He can accomplish His work through you.

In step one, I will explore the importance of reinstating God as the Chief Authority in your life. I'll identify the freedom you can experience when you banish illegitimate rulers and allow Him to sit on the throne of your heart. How can you ensure that imposters won't unseat Him? By uniting yourself with His Word and with other believers—step two of the process.

If the Lord is truly the reigning King *of* your life, His lordship will be evidenced by change *in* your life, specifically in your attitudes and actions toward others. Employers, colleagues, and subordinates should notice a difference in your behavior and your speech. Step three will urge you to make the changes God requires for Holy living.

In step four, you'll learn the value of prayer in fulfilling your commitment to accomplish both practical and spiritual tasks on the job. When God is on the throne and your efforts are covered in prayer, you can enjoy—step five—the tasks He sets before you each day. Life in Christ is anything but a drag, even at work! This kind of joy will not be affected by your circumstances; step six illustrates the true spiritual success that can be experienced in both trials and triumphs when you surrender *your will* to the *perfect will* of God the Father.

Finally, when you reach the place where your life is truly surrendered to the Chief Authority of all things, you will be able to serve the Lord most effectively, with boldness and without shame. Step seven reminds us of God's command to "go into all the world" and shine His light on people who don't yet know its warmth.

God wants you to succeed in the assignment He's given you. As you read through this devotional book, my prayer is not only that you will be left standing upright before God, but that you will emerge, even in this changing and uncertain world, with a never-ending desire to serve Him. May each step lead you to a closer and more dependent relationship with His Son, Jesus Christ—a reliable Friend who will never leave you nor forsake you. I pray you will boldly walk for Him.

> But he who looks into the perfect law of liberty and continues in
> it, and is not a forgetful hearer but a doer of the work, this one
> will be blessed in what he does. (James 1:25)

SEEK God, Your Real CEO

But seek first the kingdom of God and His righteousness, and all these things shall be added to you.

Matthew 6:33

After more than twenty years of working for other people, I am finally able to say that "those people" have no power over me.

You can say that too. You can have the peace of God that truly "surpasses all understanding" (Philippians 4:7), a peace that no tyrannical boss, conniving coworker, job merger, layoff threat, or stock-market crash can suppress. This peace adds to the quality of your life and the quantity of your faith. When you finally get it—I mean really get it, deep down in your soul—no setback will have any long-lasting effect on you ever again. That's when you'll begin to experience more joy and a greater ability to bounce back.

Here's the truth of the matter: You don't really work for your boss! You work for Jesus Christ. Your supervisor is the Holy Spirit, and you take your marching orders from the Lord. God is your CEO! Embracing that revelation will allow you to experience a new level of peace-filled freedom in your Christian walk at work. It's what the Bible terms "free indeed" (John 8:36). The key to this freedom requires each of us to strive daily, discern wisely, accept submissively, and work wholeheartedly on each assignment God sets before us.

ON ASSIGNMENT IN THE SERVICE OF THE KING

> Then Jehoiada placed the oversight of the temple of the LORD in the hands of the priests, who were Levites, to whom David had made assignments in the temple, to present the burnt offerings of the LORD as written in the Law of Moses, with rejoicing and singing, as David had ordered. (2 Chronicles 23:18, NIV)

Jehoiada was a high priest. He made the other priests supervisors, to whom David doled out temple assignments. Well, Jesus Christ is our High Priest, and He continues to give us assignments today not just in the church, but in our daily work as well. Notice that David not only ordered the Levites to carry out their assigned tasks, but he also ordered them to complete their work with "rejoicing and singing." In other words, when God chooses us to carry out an assignment and then places us in a position where He can use us, we are to be joyful. (More on that in chapter 5.)

I knew when I got the job offer at CNN that it was an assignment from the Lord. I kept saying, "Nobody gets a job like this, especially not people in my career." Let me give you a little background so you can see that, truly, the Divine is in the details.

Back in 1996 I was working as an NBC affiliate news anchor in New York City. I had made it to the number one station in the number one market for news. The position I held didn't work out for so many reasons, one of which was the Lord closing a door to open a window that was bigger than the door through which I had most recently come. (If you want all the sticky details, read my first book, *This Far by Faith: How to Put God First in Everyday Living*.)

After leaving the station, I penned *This Far by Faith* with my friend Linnie Frank. It's a book about how God, through all our ups and downs, college, careers, children, and friendship, never left us. Just writing the book became a faith-building exercise for me. I knew I had been called to complete it and then go on tour to promote it. I needed to be faithful to complete this task God had set before me, and I was. But not without financial consequence. Fourteen months after my last paycheck and six months into touring the country with the book, I was still seeking God and believing that He would come through. While supportive, all my loved ones—my husband, my mother, my father, my sister, my friends—were just a tad bit concerned. I had already borrowed from most of them and didn't know when I was going to pay them back. The mortgage was three months behind. The bill collectors knew me on a first-name basis and even pronounced my name correctly (ON-dree-ah). At regular intervals I'd hear the concerned tone in the voice of my most patient man gingerly asking, "Honey, I know you're really committed to this book and you think you're doing what God wants you to do, but when do you suppose you might go out and get...a *job?*" It's not as if I couldn't see his point. After all, he was working every day, and the reality at the time was that our lifestyle required a double income.

Some two and a half years after I had stopped working (and our financial well had nearly run bone-dry), the book tour finally wound down. I had just one more signing to go. One morning around one o'clock, I awoke from a deep sleep. My eyes opened gently, as did my spirit, and I responded to the call of the Holy Spirit. I said, "Okay, God. I hear You saying it's time. I know it's time...time to go back to work. Whatever You want me to do, wherever You want me to go, I'll go." One week later—we're talking seven days here, God's perfect number— I got a call from the then-president of CNN, who asked me to come work for him as his weekend anchor.

To this day my soul rejoices when I reflect on how faithful God was to answer the needs in my life. Living through that season increased my faith and put a new song in my heart, a song that goes something like this: *"Lord, I can always depend on You. When I obey and do what You ask me to do, I know You will see me through. I can always rejoice at what You're about to do in my life. Your Spirit leads and Your Spirit guides. I want only and always to abide in You."*

HIS WAY IS WORTHY OF OUR COMPLETE TRUST

> Trust in the LORD with all your heart,
> And lean not on your own understanding;
> In all your ways acknowledge Him,
> And He shall direct your paths. (Proverbs 3:5-6)

God is a God of completion. He always finishes what He starts. For as long as is necessary, God will bring you right back to where He first revealed Himself to you and say, "Will you trust Me?"

It seems spiritually fitting that the very first chapter of this, my second book, would bring me back to the first testing of my faith.

I had my "Seek First" experience way back in 1984. The "Seek First" principle is repeated in the gospels of Luke and Matthew, who remind us that, no matter what our circumstances look like, God will provide for all our needs if we simply seek Him first. Although I chronicled this experience in *This Far by Faith*, I believe the principle is important enough to repeat here.

The thing I have come to know about God's way of blessing us is what the church ladies have said for generations: "He may not come when you want Him, but He's always on time." Understanding and accepting my Lord's perfect timing has given me peace of mind. Even when I've had no idea of how a particular challenge would be resolved,

I've still had peace. Why? Because I remain confident in His promise that He will never leave me alone.

A true turning point in my faith journey came when I was twenty-seven years old. I had just taken a job as news anchor and reporter in New Orleans. I went there knowing that I was taking a step back in order to take two steps forward. It was a risk I needed to take in hopes of advancing my career as a journalist.

I had been there only two months when, through "celestial serendipity," I was given the opportunity to go to work on a great local news magazine program in Boston. The Boston job would double my salary and move me into a top-ten market. It offered greater exposure, travel, and the chance to be closer to my family. I went there one weekend, had an interview, and was offered the job. Who could hold me back from such a wonderful blessing? Unfortunately, there was a small glitch: I had just signed a two-year contract with the New Orleans station.

I went and had a talk with my boss. I told him of the Boston offer, how excited I was, and what a rare opportunity had been placed before me. I apologized and asked if he would release me from my contract. I expected him to say, "Oh, Andria, I understand. You know I only want the best for you. Go, my child, go north with my blessings." Why I expected him to respond in such a way, I'll never know. What he said instead was, "No!" The station had paid for my moving expenses down to Louisiana. They had put me up in a hotel for a month while I found an apartment. They had made a considerable investment in hiring me.

Well, there I was: stuck. The news director was not going to let me out of my contract. Then it got worse. The program director in Boston rescinded his offer, citing a phone call from the New Orleans station threatening to sue them for tampering with my contract. What was I to do? I couldn't fathom working for the next two years at a station that wanted to stymie my professional growth. (Such was my perception at the time.) I had to make a decision. The Boston station told me that if I somehow found myself unemployed and the job were still available, it was mine, but they could no longer actively pursue the hire. The New Orleans station now knew I was no longer committed in the way I had been when I came on board. I sought the Lord and decided to leave. I was going to have to take a chance with no promises on the other side of that risk.

When I'm in the dark, clueless about where I'm going or what I should do, I simply open the Bible and let the pages turn where they may. That night, I let the Spirit lead me to this scripture in Luke 12:27-28 (NIV): "Consider how the lilies grow. They do not labor or spin. Yet I tell you, not even Solomon in all his splendor was dressed like one of these. If that is how God clothes the grass of the field, which is here today, and tomorrow is thrown into the fire, how much more will he clothe you!"

There it was in black and white. I knew then that God would provide. Just moments earlier, I had been worried sick about how I would make ends meet. But after reading the scripture, I chose to stop worrying, believe His Word, and step out on faith. The next day I let the television station in New Orleans know I would be leaving. For the first time in my career, I would be without a paycheck and without a professional platform. I stood firm on the promises of God and moved forward not knowing the specific outcome of all I had hoped. But Hebrews 11:1 reminds us that "faith is the substance of things hoped for, the evidence of things not seen." I hoped I could still land that job in Boston, yet I had no proof it would be available to me once I closed the door on my current job.

Well, walking by faith and not by sight paid off. I got the job in Beantown and worked there for nearly ten years. Clearly, divine intervention had placed me on a road I was meant to travel. For someone else in her unique situation, God may have said not to break the contract and to stick it out, but in my situation, God's leading was clear. That job was the most professionally satisfying work experience I have had until now. The road led me to marriage and the blessing of children. My faith was rewarded because I believed what God said instead of what my circumstances dictated. I trusted in His Word. I will always stand on His promises.

The Heart Is Like Clay in the Hands of the Lord

> The king's heart is in the hand of the LORD,
> Like the rivers of water;
> He turns it wherever He wishes. (Proverbs 21:1)

Consider how my heavenly CEO worked out all the details of my job situation to the benefit of everyone involved. All I did was stand there in awe of what God chose to do. The Lord moved the heart of the Boston program director to extend a buyout offer to my former New Orleans employer. That means the Boston station purchased my contract from the station in New Orleans, even though they weren't legally obligated to do so. Everyone was compensated, and no one lost out.

Wow! I am so thankful that God met me right where I was according to my level of faith and spiritual maturity. He will meet you, too, right where you are. While my intentions at that time were admittedly a bit selfish, God's intention in that situation was to grow my faith. It worked! And in the meantime I learned several important lessons:

- God will creatively bless us when our trust gives Him room to do so.
- It is imperative that we examine our motives in light of God's Word, so that in our desire to be blessed we don't unintentionally set up someone else to be burdened. What I've learned

since my New Orleans' experience is to remember that it's
not only about us. God wants our hearts to be big enough
to consider how our actions will affect others.

- The counsel of God will guide us if we seek it. And if we
  don't, His desire for us will prevail anyway! "Listen to advice
  and accept instruction, and in the end you will be wise. Many
  are the plans in a man's heart, but it is the LORD's purpose that
  prevails" (Proverbs 19:20-21, NIV).

Practical Application

Ask, and it will be given to you; seek, and you will find; knock,
and it will be opened to you. For everyone who asks receives, and
he who seeks finds, and to him who knocks it will be opened.
(Matthew 7:7-8)

- *Ask* God for His direction.
- *Seek* what He wants in your life by spending time in prayer,
  reading His Word, and soliciting the counsel of godly advisors.
- *Knock* on the doors of opportunity as God sets them in front
  of you.

Spiritual Truth

And God is able to make all grace abound toward you, that
you, always having all sufficiency in all things, may have an
abundance for every good work. (2 Corinthians 9:8)

We will never lose when we go with God!

First Steps

- Ask the Holy Spirit to reveal to you your particular assignment in the place where you work. Pray for direction and
  then find a scripture from the Holy Bible to motivate you
  to stay on course. You might, for instance, choose, "Bond-
  servants, obey in all things your masters according to the flesh,
  not with eyeservice, as men-pleasers, but in sincerity of heart,
  fearing God. And whatever you do, do it heartily, as to the
  Lord and not to men, knowing that from the Lord you will
  receive the reward of the inheritance; for you serve the Lord
  Christ" (Colossians 3:22-24).
- Look for patterns in what you are consistently called to do by
  either your employer or your colleagues. Begin to track these
  on your journal pages.
- Confess in prayer: "I am a vessel of God" (see Romans
  9:21-24). Invite the Lord to clean you up, making you a
  vessel of honor through whom He can shine His light into
  your workplace.

Journal Exercises

Write down the scripture God pressed upon your heart in "First Steps."
Once a week over the course of this month, write down what God is
revealing to you in light of this scripture about the assignment He has
given you. Print the scripture on colorful stationery in bold, beautiful
letters. Frame your scripture and commit it to memory. Make it a peri-
odic goal (for example, monthly or annually) to ask God for a new scripture whenever He begins to do a new work in you (see Isaiah 43:19).

Your Plan Is My Prayer

Lord God, Your plan is my prayer.

Sweet Jesus, Your will is my way.

Holy Spirit, Your direction for my life

Is the only thing that matters to me now.

I'm so tired of playing by "the rules,"

Knowing that the way of this world is not Yours.

You said to be in the world, but not of it.

How do I do that when all the trappings around me
    point me in a direction

Other than where You are?

I do it first by seeking Your agenda, Lord God,

Searching and seeking to serve You in spirit and in truth.

That means I must present myself in right standing.

Just like Zacharias and Elizabeth of old, who walked in
    all the commandments

And were blameless before You, Lord, I, too, want to do
    Your will

In Your way and wait patiently for Your timing.

You promise, when I seek You first and Your righteous-
    ness, I will never have to worry about my needs
    again. I will be free to serve You right where I am.

I know, Lord, that You've got me covered! And that is a
    comfort to me today and every day.

In the name of Jesus, I pray.

Amen.

AUTHORITY

Then Jesus came to them and said, "All authority in heaven and on earth has been given to me."

MATTHEW 28:18, NIV

Jesus Christ is in charge of my life. And the Word says I must worship Him "in spirit and truth" (John 4:24). In acknowledging these truths, I realize that my first spiritual key to success requires me to trust in what I do not see—the spiritual realm—more than in what I do see—the physical realm. God is Spirit, and these are the facts according to the Holy Bible: Jesus Christ is Lord! My boss is not in charge. I am not in charge. God is in charge!

After Jesus was crucified and resurrected, His disciples saw their risen Lord, and they worshiped at His feet. But even then some doubted. What did Jesus do? Did He raise His voice in anger or frustration and say, "What's it going to take for you guys to get it?" No. He simply and calmly stated the facts: "All authority in heaven and on earth has been given to me."

People who truly have authority don't have to scream it out. They don't have to pummel people over the head with what they want. If I have true authority, I just speak the truth without buying into the insecurities of others. Eventually, the truth has a way of setting the record straight. God is my ultimate Authority. I do not fear men or what they might do to me. If I make sure my walk is right with God, then I am assured daily that I am on the right path, no matter what things look like.

Action Point: Today I confess from my mouth that God is the Authority over my life (see Romans 10:9-10).

ALMIGHTY FATHER

Yes, the Almighty will be your gold, and your precious silver; for then you will have your delight in the Almighty, and lift up your face to God.

JOB 22:25-26

Do I believe work is only about power and the almighty dollar? Simply put, it's about the Almighty Father, and I am to be about my Father's business (see Luke 2:49). When Jesus was just twelve years old, He lingered behind in the temple seeking knowledge, asking questions, and revealing to the scholars even then that He was worthy of their attention. What happened after that? "Jesus increased in wisdom and stature, and in favor with God and men" (Luke 2:52).

When I focus on God's plan and not my own, amazing things happen. I gain wisdom, acquire stature, and find favor with both Almighty God and men. No one is saying it is easy, but it is simple. The first thing I must do is seek the wisdom of the Holy Spirit daily, enrolling myself in His school of spiritual training. I think of it as an investment in my career. By spending time in His Word, by committing to daily prayer and meditation, I can expect God to speak to me. I believe He wants to reveal to me His plan for my life at work. My responsibility is to discipline myself to be on the lookout for His purposes in everyday situations. Perhaps this day my coworker needs a word of encouragement. Perhaps my boss needs me to go the extra mile. Maybe the light that is bursting forth in me will be the light that leads someone to Jesus.

Action Point: Today I remember that the Almighty is calling me to be about *His* business.

BELIEF

Now He did not do many mighty works there because of their unbelief.

MATTHEW 13:58

My belief is the key to unlocking the many mighty works of Jesus. It has nothing to do with His ability and everything to do with my willingness to let Him be Lord of my life, especially at the office. I know that God is anxious to strut His stuff for me at work. He wants to brighten my light. He wants to build my faith by displaying His awesome works, for which I can take absolutely no credit; I can simply give Him the glory.

Therefore, this day I cry out to the Lord, as did the man recorded in Mark 9, who stood in the midst of the crowd, longing for the Son of God to heal his child. I realize that each time I am confronted with the seemingly impossible Jesus asks me whether I can believe Him. "If you can believe, all things are possible to him who believes" (verse 23). My response to Him must be the same as that brokenhearted and convicted man who wanted the Master's miracles but knew his own issues were holding him back. "Immediately the father of the child cried out and said with tears, 'Lord, I believe; help my unbelief!'" (verse 24). Notice that the man *immediately* cried out to God. He recognized his belief level was not where it should have been.

Action Point: Today, as my faith fails, I ask the Holy Spirit to convict me, so I cry out to You, dear Jesus, "Lord, I believe; help my unbelief!"

BOREDOM

Have you not known? Have you not heard? The everlasting God,
the LORD, the Creator of the ends of the earth, neither faints nor is
weary. His understanding is unsearchable. He gives power to the
weak, and to those who have no might He increases strength.

ISAIAH 40:28-29

Why am I bored? Perhaps I have been at this job too long. Maybe I'm just weary from laboring all my life. Okay, so boredom is not a crime, but it is a condition, a condition that can be fixed only by the Lord.

Listen: "Have you not known? Have you not heard?" In other words, "Where have you been? Have you buried your head in the sand? C'mon, you're a believer, right? You know God is the Alpha and the Omega. Everything starts with Him and everything ends with Him. So why not take even this to Him?" Isaiah reminds me that though I may grow tired, God never does. In fact, He sustains me by His gifts of power and increased strength. So, when I feel completely *bored,* tired of laboring, weary from the nine-to-five routine day in and day out, I will remember…to turn. Turn to God, "the Creator of the ends of the earth." Yes, God can handle my boredom.

Dear Lord, I know that Your understanding is unsearchable in every situation. So even though right now I feel as if I can't take another day of the same old thing, I focus instead on the fact that You will increase my ability to bear all things. Even when I'm feeling disinterested and disturbed, You will give me the power to endure.

Action Point: Today I look for signs of God's presence in the mundane, knowing that often the divine is in the details.

AUTHENTICITY

Jesus answered, "My teaching is not my own. It comes from him who sent me. If anyone chooses to do God's will, he will find out whether my teaching comes from God or whether I speak on my own. He who speaks on his own does so to gain honor for himself, but he who works for the honor of the one who sent him is a man of truth; there is nothing false about him."

JOHN 7:16-18, NIV

When Jesus walked and talked and healed people, He in no way sought to draw attention to Himself. Amidst all the oohs and ahhs, He never once said, "Look at Me. If you thought that was something, watch this!" Lord God, let me follow Jesus' example of always seeking to do Your will for Your glory and always aiming to live according to Your truth.

I've heard American journalists throw around the phrase *truth in reporting*. It's an ethical principle throughout the industry to report just the facts when covering a story. Such journalism jobs are easy compared to the one I'm setting my mind to do. Every day I am covering The Story, the one God is writing of my life. I am reporting on it to others through what I say, how I act, and most of all in what I do. I don't ever want to be a fake. I want to be the real deal, used by Him at anytime and in anyway.

Lord, let me not be like the treacherous Judah of old, who did not turn to You with her whole heart, but instead did so in pretense (see Jeremiah 3:10). Search my heart, Father. Look closely at my intentions. Place them under Your heavenly microscope, and whatever You find that is not authentic, take it out and start the process of purifying me once again.

Action Point: Today before I speak or act, I will think, *For the honor of Him who sent me...*

DEDICATION

Nevertheless Asa's heart was loyal to the LORD all his days. He also brought into the house of the LORD the things which his father had dedicated, and the things which he himself had dedicated: silver and gold and utensils.

1 KINGS 15:14-15

Lord, cleanse my heart. I want to be loyal to You all the days of my life. So this day I start afresh by dedicating to You my time, my talents, my self. I acknowledge that it is only by Your grace and goodness that I have what I have. In You I live and move and have my being (see Acts 17:28).

So, if I get weak or weary today, I will stop and find a place to pray. I will say to You once again, "I give to You this challenge, this moment, this madness I find myself in." I know "that all things work together for good to those who love God, to those who are called according to His purpose" (Romans 8:28).

Call me, sweet Jesus. Call me, dear Lord. I dedicate and will daily rededicate my life, my work, and my all to You. The silver of my hands, the gold of my heart, and the utensils of my talent—let these be a start. Use me, Lord, this day to speak into the life of another. I want others to see that I gladly serve a living God whose good pleasure it is to give me His kingdom (see Luke 12:32). When my life is wholly devoted to You, You will fill my life with more than I could ever have imagined or expected.

Action Point: Today I dedicate each problem, each blessing, and each opportunity to the Lord for His glory and my good.

EGOTISM

But know this, that in the last days perilous times will come: For men will be lovers of themselves, lovers of money, boasters, proud, blasphemers, disobedient to parents, unthankful, unholy, unloving, unforgiving, slanderers, without self-control, brutal, despisers of good, traitors, headstrong, haughty, lovers of pleasure rather than lovers of God.

2 TIMOTHY 3:1-4

Having an ego is one thing; practicing *egotism* is quite another. The latter is a sin. I do not have to look very far to see the signs that we are in perilous times. It is especially apparent in the workplace. People all around me love all the wrong things: themselves, money, power, and prestige. I feel surrounded by those who are unappreciative, have no self-control, or are constantly using the Lord's name in a curse.

At times I, too, fall into this category of egotistical people. When I look within myself hard enough and honestly enough, I don't have to look very far to see the signs. Lord, sometimes I am headstrong and haughty, and I enjoy the things of this world just a little too much. God forbid that these become the object of my affection more than You, Lord. Let me keep my ego in check, and, Lord, please keep me from loving myself more than I love You.

Action Point: Today I focus on a quality in the scripture above and—rooted in humility and service to God—look for ways to demonstrate its opposite by my thoughts and actions.

ELOHIM

In the beginning God...

GENESIS 1:1

While I may know the name of my company president, and while I may know the names of a host of professional contacts, this is the Name I really want to remember: *Elohim*. It is the Hebrew word that we translate "God." It is also a name—beyond my comprehension—that says much about who God really is. Many linguistic scholars have determined that Elohim is written in the plural form. Yes, my God exists in the plural. He is the Father, the Son, and the Holy Spirit wrapped into One. The Trinity upon which I stand and depend. The Alpha and Omega, my beginning and my end. He is Sovereign Lord and Master of humanity.

Elohim: God of gods, Lord of lords.

Elohim: All powerful, mighty, and strong.

Elohim: Omnipotent and omnipresent.

Elohim: Supreme and faithful Creator. Who else is there?

What a blessing to know God as Elohim! Today I can say and be assured: Elohim, You will guide me. Elohim, You will protect me with Your mighty, strong, and powerful hand. Elohim, You will hear me. Yes, for You are faithful in Your promise never to leave me or forsake me (see Joshua 1:5).

Action Point: Today if I feel weak and insecure, I call upon Elohim and draw strength in knowing God can and will creatively work all things together for good!

FAITH

*Now faith is the substance of things hoped for, the evidence of things
not seen.*

HEBREWS 11:1

No matter what, today my *faith* in God will see me through. I don't
have to know the outcome of a particular situation. I don't have to have
all the details. I don't even have to be included in every meeting or be
kept in the loop concerning the company's latest mandates. All I have to
do is have a little bit of *faith*.

Some days my faith is the size of Mount Everest. Other days I have
a pretty hard time scraping together just a few little mustard seeds, but
even that's okay because all I have to come up with today is a single tiny
seed. "If you have faith as a mustard seed, you will say to this mountain,
'Move from here to there,' and it will move; and nothing will be impossible for you" (Matthew 17:20). All things are possible through faith.
Nothing can keep me from moving my mountains today.

F is for First. The first thing I must do today is pray.

A is for Almighty. Second, I must remember that He's got it
   under control.

I is for "I AM." Third, I must call out His name.

T is for Tower of Strength. Fourth, I must remember that Jesus
   is my strength, so I can stand through all of life's challenges.

H is for Hope. Fifth, I must cling to joy, which is founded in
   Him and not in my circumstances.

Action Point: Today I fuel my faith by searching God's Word, knowing that the living water in it will grow my mustard seed of faith into a
mountain of belief.

FOUNDATION

For no other foundation can anyone lay than that which is laid, which is Jesus Christ.

1 CORINTHIANS 3:11

A house is only as strong as the foundation on which it is built. Build a house on sand, and it will sink. Build a house on a firm foundation, and it will stand not only the test of time but also the forces of nature.

My personal hope and professional house are built on the revelation that apart from Jesus Christ, I have no hope. With Him I can do all things (see Philippians 4:13). Daily I make sure that my foundation is firm, so that when others look at my house, they will marvel at its strength. They will marvel at its staying power. I will marvel at the majesty and grace afforded me through the Son of God, who came so that I might have life—"and have it more abundantly" (John 10:10).

So, if life gets difficult this day, I will remember that I am standing on a firm Foundation. If others demand too much of me today, I will remember my Foundation and call out to Him for help. If I am stressed and tired from the week I have just endured, I will remember that my Foundation not only endured all things unto death but also rose again so that I, too, might rise. Let me lift my head high right now and look to Him, "from whence comes my help" (Psalm 121:1). I rejoice, for I have a Foundation who will never fall nor fail.

Action Point: Today I won't be afraid when the storms of life wash over me—because my foundation is Christ, and He will hold me up.

GOALS

After beginning with the Spirit, are you now trying to attain your goal by human effort?

GALATIANS 3:3, NIV

The moment I align my goals with the goals of God for my life, I will find myself on the path to godly success.

I often pray for guidance, ask for help, and then, when Help comes, think, *I can take it from here,* but the Holy Spirit wants a different response. Haven't I learned the hard way yet? I keep trying and trying. I keep moving by my own power without getting very far, but the Word of God says, "Not by might nor by power, but by My Spirit" (Zechariah 4:6).

Therefore:

- My first goal today is to work with the Spirit of God. Lord, by the power of Your Holy Spirit, show me what You want to accomplish through me this day.

- My second goal is to bring into my environment the light of the Lord and the peace that only He can give (see John 14:27). Lord, I thank You for leaving me Your peace.

- My third goal today is to share a praise report with someone. Lord, even if it is only a little something You've done for me this day, no blessing is too small to praise You openly. For You are worthy to be praised, and Your name shall continually be in my mouth (see Hebrews 13:15). Lord, You and You alone are worthy of my praise.

Action Point: Today I take the first step of aligning my goals with God's goals for me by asking Him to reveal what He wants at the top of my to-do list.

HEARER

If anyone is a hearer of the word and not a doer, he is like a man observing his natural face in a mirror; for he observes himself, goes away, and immediately forgets what kind of man he was.

JAMES 1:23-24

How many times have I gone to church on Sunday morning looking for "a word"? I say, "Lord, please speak to me. Speak to my heart." The Holy Spirit moves and answers my request. My faith is strengthened, renewed, and revived. Then Monday rolls around, and I somehow put that word from God in a box somewhere with a note attached: *For use after work hours only.* Sometimes I never even open my spiritual treasure chest until the following Sunday, when I go back for my weekly dose of doctrine. Guilty as charged! Guilty of placing restrictions on God. Guilty of not connecting Sunday to Monday. Guilty of being a hearer of the Word, not a doer of the Word.

What would my life be like if I examined myself in a mirror, studied all the intimate details of who I am, walked away, and then— *boom!*—didn't remember a single thing about what I look like? Well, if I am only about hearing on Sunday and not about doing on Monday, Lord, take me back and convict me with your Word.

Action Point: Today I make a physical note of what I hear from the Lord and post it in a place to remind me to do something in response.

HUMILITY

Then their father Israel said to them, "If it must be, then do this:
Put some of the best products of the land in your bags and take
them down to the man as a gift—a little balm and a little honey,
some spices and myrrh, some pistachio nuts and almonds."

GENESIS 43:11, NIV

Israel's choice to humble himself and his family before Joseph, the second most powerful man in Egypt after the king, reminds me that seeking God's will requires me to humble myself before God and to bring to my relationship with Him the very best I have to offer, my "firstfruits" (Deuteronomy 26:9-10). It's not as if God needs anything I can give—no more than Joseph needed Israel's gifts—but God loves a cheerful giver and will search my heart to see if I am willing to give Him my very best. Certainly He gave me His.

When God saw that the world needed a Savior, He sent His only Son for me. When God saw that I was flawed and sinful, He sent nothing less than Divinity. When God saw my faults and helplessness, He sent for me Hope and Righteousness.

I will never be perfect in anything I do. Not at home, not at work, not in life or love or truth. But I know One who is perfect, and just the mention of His name makes me thank God for sending His sweet Son Jesus, whom I can gratefully claim as my Savior, and without whom I am nothing.

Action Point: Because God is worthy of the best I have to offer, I thank Him for what He has done for me and make every effort today to humbly do my work as unto Him.

FIRST THINGS FIRST

Seek first the kingdom of God and His righteousness, and all these things shall be added to you.

MATTHEW 6:33

Why do I work anyway? Do I work for the money? for the status? for God?

Unfortunately, I live in a society where, for many, what we do becomes who we are. That is a lie of the world that leaves anyone who buys into it clinging to a life raft, adrift on the world's raging sea. This lie fosters the wrong motivation and certainly the wrong attitude. When I begin to define myself by a title or a certain salary level, I risk changing who I am every time I change jobs. But God never changes (see Malachi 3:6), and when I root my identity in Him, I don't have to either. I want Him to be my incentive for getting up every morning.

No question, if I didn't get paid, I might not show up. Even so, I don't want my paycheck to be my sole incentive for being available to God in the workplace. Furthermore, I want my goal to be the same as His: I will seek to build His kingdom and seek His righteousness for my life. Now that's a pretty high standard, and I will never be as holy as my Lord and Savior Jesus Christ, who "was in all points tempted" as I have been, "yet without sin" (Hebrews 4:15). But when I pursue holiness, I can go about my life without anxiety, paycheck or none. "Therefore do not worry, saying, 'What shall we eat?' or 'What shall we drink?' or 'What shall we wear?'...For your heavenly Father knows that you need all these things" (Matthew 6:31-32).

Action Point: Today I seek God first, trusting that all other things shall be added to me.

KINGDOM LIVING

> *But when they believed Philip as he preached the things concerning the kingdom of God and the name of Jesus Christ, both men and women were baptized. Then Simon himself also believed; and when he was baptized he continued with Philip, and was amazed, seeing the miracles and signs which were done.*
>
> ACTS 8:12-13

Seeking first "the kingdom of God and His righteousness" (Matthew 6:33) means in part living in such a way that others know I am a follower of Christ.

I want my life to be a living testament to Him. I want my walk with Christ—especially at the office—to be an example of Christian behavior to others. I want to encourage believers to walk worthy of their calling (see Ephesians 4:1). I want nonbelievers to see Christ in me, so that maybe they will also seek His kingdom and be transformed.

When I open my Bible to Acts 8, I see how a man named Simon was changed overnight from practicing false doctrine, claiming that he was someone great, to becoming a follower of Christ—and, by God's grace, this change came when Simon observed the behavior of Philip, a preacher of the gospel. Simon the proud became humbled and amazed at all he had seen at work in the life of one man. It is my hope that others are similarly amazed when they see what the Lord is doing in mine.

Action Point: Today I read Acts 8:9-25 and remember that I am not great, but rather it is God in me who is great.

KNOWLEDGE OF GOD

Let no arrogance come from your mouth, for the LORD is the God of knowledge; and by Him actions are weighed.

1 SAMUEL 2:3

Oftentimes when people immerse themselves in the "things of the world," they get cocky. They walk around with arrogance, acting as if blessings are the result of their own achievements rather than a gift from the Lord. God has no problem with any of His children being richly blessed, for we know that "every good and every perfect gift is from above" (James 1:17). God, however, wants the credit, for He is a jealous God, and there are to be no other gods before Him (see Exodus 20:3).

I might think I have "arrived" because I'm so smart and I'm just that good, but this mode of thinking is foolishness to God (see 1 Corinthians 3:19). For He and He alone is the God of knowledge, and His Word says: "The fear of the LORD is the beginning of wisdom, and the knowledge of the Holy One is understanding" (Proverbs 9:10).

Let me, therefore, seek to know Him, learn of Him (see Matthew 11:29), and understand who He is. If I truly want knowledge, then I must understand the mind of Christ and measure myself by that, not by vain imaginations and puffed-up pride (see 1 Corinthians 2:15-16). Knowledge comes after wisdom. When I pray for wisdom and confidently receive it (see James 1:5), then I will understand what it means to fear the Lord—not as in "I'm shaking in my boots," but as in understanding that He holds *all* the cards, and if I know anything at all, that reality check should move me to a place of abiding humility.

Action Point: Today as I face trouble, I ask God to reveal to me the mind of Christ in my circumstances.

Fruitful Labor

Unless the LORD builds the house, they labor in vain who build it;
unless the LORD guards the city, the watchman stays awake in vain.

PSALM 127:1

There's a saying, "If the Lord is your copilot, you need to switch seats." How many times do I say, "If it's Your will, Father, let it be done," but then go forward with *my* plans? How often do I work hard for the things I want for my own life without firmly establishing, through prayer and counsel, whether my desires align with God's? I may pray like a copilot, but I'm steering the plane nevertheless.

Lord, help me get to the point where I can honestly say, "I don't want anything for my life that You don't want for me." Frankly, I get tired of laboring in vain because I am striving for the wrong things. I find myself exhausted from applying the skill, talent, and time You have afforded me—only to realize later that I have been fighting a tide that is rolling in another direction.

Build me up, Lord, and build my house. If my "house" is a project or a physical building, or if my house is a longtime desire or a material possession to acquire—Lord, only You can create Your best for me and then enable me to give it right back to You. I want everything I labor for to bring You glory. If it doesn't, Lord, dismantle my desires and start all over again in me. Maybe next time I'll get it right from the start and let You draw up the master plan. I'll follow your plan and get with Your program. I believe order brings victory, which is far better than laboring in vain.

Action Point: Today I ask God to begin to dismantle dreams that are not from Him so that He can replace those with His dreams for me.

"LORD!"

But why do you call Me "Lord, Lord," and not do the things which I say?

LUKE 6:46

Oh, how easy it is to call on the name of Jesus when I am in trouble…

Stress at the office? Personalities and politics pushing me to the wall? When I feel I can't handle things anymore myself, that's likely to be the time when I cry out, "Lord, what do You want me to do?" Jesus' response: "Why do you call My name and then still go on doing your own thing?"

Lord, forgive me. I want to put You first in all things, yet I forget that You want to handle it *all,* and handle it from the start. From the biggest to the smallest. This meeting, that report; this person, that retort. I must bring it *all* to You. Nothing is too little or too big to give over to You in prayer, for You are faithful to respond.

It is one thing to see You as my Savior and another to see You as my Lord. When You are Lord of my life, I consciously give You permission to have Your way with me. So, Lord, this day, I start over again, first by calling You Lord and then by handing everything over to You. I know I can cast my cares on You and You will sustain me, never permitting "the righteous to be moved" (Psalm 55:22).

Action Point: Today I begin my day with a prayer acknowledging Christ as Lord over *all* in my life. I trust in His sovereign will for me.

POWER

But you shall receive power when the Holy Spirit has come upon you; and you shall be witnesses to Me in Jerusalem, and in all Judea and Samaria, and to the end of the earth.

ACTS 1:8

When I say, "Thank God for Jesus," I add to that, "Thank You, Jesus, for praying that Your Holy Spirit would come for me, for without Him I would not be able to work or live victoriously." Jesus told His disciples, "If you love Me, keep My commandments. And I will pray the Father, and He will give you another Helper, that He may abide with you forever" (John 14:15-16).

Now, that is power! Power literally from on high. Power that I can call upon at this very moment and in this very situation. The Holy Spirit is His name. He is a Person and a Force, and He is available to me—in fact, He lives in me—because I am a believer. If I want to tap into His power, I must be pleasing in His sight, remembering that for every provision I receive from God there is a condition I must meet.

When I look at the above scripture from John, I see that Jesus said: "If you love Me, keep my commandments. And…" Let me back up and read that again. I see that access to the Holy Spirit is linked directly to my love and obedience to Christ. When I meet the condition of love and obedience, then Jesus intercedes for me, igniting the Holy Spirit to help me and abide with me not just in the here and now, but forever. Lord, let me walk daily in obedience to You, so that with confidence I can ask the *Holy Spirit* for help and receive it by faith.

Action Point: Today I choose obedience to the Lord over my fleshly desires.

POSSIBILITIES

But Jesus looked at them and said to them, "With men this is im-
possible, but with God all things are possible."

MATTHEW 19:26

Today is a day for possibilities! Today is a day for accepting my position and place in the world as a child of the Most High King. When I prepare for work, I must realize that when my walk with Christ is correct, the Spirit of the living God can work through me no matter what challenges I confront when I step through the doors of my workplace. When I am in right standing before the Lord, it isn't just me talking, but God speaking words of life through me. If I am completely sold out for Jesus, then when I find myself at work, I have two jobs to do: The first is to perform to the best of my abilities; the second is to point the way to Him and to a blessed life of *possibilities*. "Eye has not seen, nor ear heard, nor have entered into the heart of man the things which God has prepared for those who love Him" (1 Corinthians 2:9).

It is possible for me to make someone smile today. It is possible to change someone's attitude today. It's even possible for me to show someone the Way today, the way to the only One who can save. His name is Jesus, and because of Him, my days are filled with possibilities.

Action Point: Today I live a life of possibilities, knowing that on my own I can only accomplish so much, but with God all things are possible.

UNITE Yourself with the Word and Other Believers

For everything that was written in the past was written to teach us, so that through endurance and the encouragement of the Scriptures we might have hope. May the God who gives endurance and encouragement give you a spirit of unity among yourselves as you follow Christ Jesus, so that with one heart and mouth you may glorify the God and Father of our Lord Jesus Christ. Accept one another, then, just as Christ accepted you, in order to bring praise to God.

ROMANS 15:4-7, NIV

Have you ever reflected on where you've been, where you're going, and where you are right now—only to ask yourself, *How on earth did I get here?* At some point in our careers, most of us have asked ourselves that same question. But I believe the real question is: *How in heaven...?* As I mentioned in chapter 1, every job I have ever had has clearly been divinely ordered. No opportunity has ever been solely orchestrated by me, although I would love to take credit. The only thing I've ever done is prepare myself for the moments when God has placed an opportunity before me and then followed through with what He asked me to do.

You've heard the saying, "If you take one step, He'll take two." Well, God definitely expects us to get with the program when He directs us. The biggest challenge most of us have in seeking God is knowing when

God is talking. Knowing when God is moving. Knowing when God is guiding us.

God speaks to us and guides us in three major ways, through:

- His Word—the *Holy* Bible.
- His *Holy* Spirit.
- *holy* men and women of God called into kingdom service.

As we seek the will of God in difficult on-the-job situations, being attuned to God's voice in these three elements is of critical importance.

THE ONLY SELF-HELP BOOK YOU'LL EVER NEED

> Moreover, brethren, I declare to you the gospel which I preached
> to you, which also you received and in which you stand, by which
> also you are saved, if you hold fast that word which I preached to
> you—unless you believed in vain. (1 Corinthians 15:1-2)

Have you ever considered how much money you've spent on self-help manuals and tools? Let's face it, there are so many self-help books out there, you need help just to sort through them all. Now there's an idea: *A Book to Help You Find the Right Self-Help Book.* Okay, a little sarcasm, but you get my point.

With the plethora of help available to us—some good and some questionable—what's even more amazing is that all we ever need is contained between the two covers of God's ultimate self-help manual. And unlike many of the world's guidebooks, it contains absolutely reliable advice.

Are you telling me, Andria, that I didn't really need to read all of those self-help manuals? You got it!

- Instead of *How to Succeed in Business Without Ever Working for It,* we know, "If anyone will not work, neither shall he eat" (2 Thessalonians 3:10).

- Instead of *How to Succeed in Life by Being the God of Your Life*, Scripture assures us "For if we live, we live to the Lord; and if we die, we die to the Lord. Therefore, whether we live or die, we are the Lord's" (Romans 14:8).
- Instead of *How to Succeed in Communicating Without Ever Talking*, we hear, "Then those who feared the LORD talked with each other, and the LORD listened and heard" (Malachi 3:16, NIV).

Life would be so much simpler if we could just hang with this concept: All the wisdom of man could never match the wisdom of God. "For the wisdom of this world is foolishness with God. For it is written, 'He catches the wise in their own craftiness'; and again, 'The LORD knows the thoughts of the wise, that they are futile'" (1 Corinthians 3:19-20).

When we go to the Source, when we use the Word of God as the definitive self-help tool, we basically skip the middleman. Now, don't get me wrong, I'm not looking for you to close *this book* right now! My point is simply this: Everything we need for success has already been written. It is already done. It is finished! God is Jehovah-Jireh, the Lord who provides. He has and He does! We can take advantage of God's provision by reading, absorbing, and then daily applying His truth to our immediate circumstances. His Word is indeed our *daily bread.* "And Jesus said to them, 'I am the bread of life. He who comes to Me shall never hunger, and he who believes in Me shall never thirst'" (John 6:35). If we are to walk with purpose, power, and perseverance, it is imperative that we understand this key spiritual principle: *The depth of our relationship with Jesus is directly related to the discipline we exercise in studying God's Word.* Why? Jesus is the Word! He always was and forever shall be (see John 1:1-2).

When we stay close to God's instruction Book, the Holy Bible, our thoughts and opinions radiate His truth. People respond to and respect the truth. God responds to and blesses us when we walk in truth.

If you abide in Me, and My words abide in you, you will ask
what you desire, and it shall be done for you. (John 15:7)

There is a mystery in John 15, and I've just given you a major piece
of the puzzle. If you want to successfully walk for Christ, much of your
success hinges on connecting the following biblical dots.

- Jesus is the Word (see John 1:1-5).
- The Word is a life-sustaining vine (see John 15:5).
- If we are to thrive, we must stay connected to that vine
  (see John 15:4).
- We must abide in the Word (see John 15:7).

We must stand on the Word!

If We Stand on the Word, They Won't Be Able to Push Us over the Edge

These things we also speak, not in words which man's wisdom
teaches but which the Holy Spirit teaches, comparing spiritual things
with spiritual. But the natural man does not receive the things of the
Spirit of God, for they are foolishness to him; nor can he know
them, because they are spiritually discerned. (1 Corinthians 2:13-14)

Ever work with someone, day in and day out, who may be nice enough
but who absolutely, positively gets on your last nerve? Ever work some-
place where, almost before you get in the door, you can feel a headache
coming on because there's so much stress waiting for you? Maybe you
constantly sing the spiritual "He Knows How Much I Can Bear." You
know you want to leave the job—you've been there way too long anyway—and every day you go in and wonder why you're still there.

There are just some people, some assignments, and some jobs that truly challenge you to be Christlike on a daily basis. If you are at a job where you often feel fatigued, frustrated, and infuriated, this is a sure sign that you need to "set your mind on things above, not on things on the earth" (Colossians 3:2). God wants to actively join you at work, but realize this: The Holy Spirit is a gentleman. He won't force Himself on anyone, but if we treat Him with respect and reverence, we will find He is the perfect escort. Simply open your heart and say, "Holy Spirit, have Your way." He will.

The only way to triumph daily at the office and in life is to stand! *Stand* firmly on the Word of God. If we rely on any other manual that promises life and success, we'll fail. Remember, we Christians live by a different standard, a higher standard. It's not that those self-help books don't work. Many are actually based on biblical principles. But they don't attribute what truth they may contain to the Source, and we need that Source to guide us daily. We, my friends, are going to do this work thing by *the* Book: the Holy Bible.

Spiritual things/truths must be spiritually discerned (see 1 Corinthians 2:13-14). God's Word is not complicated; it is *revealed.* From the moment I understood this, I began to ask Him for spiritual discernment. What a concept! James told Christ's followers, "If any of you lacks wisdom, he should ask God, who gives generously to all without finding fault, and it will be given to him" (James 1:5, NIV).

Getting Angry with Our Real Enemy

Be self-controlled and alert. Your enemy the devil prowls
around like a roaring lion looking for someone to devour.
Resist him, standing firm in the faith, because you know that
your brothers throughout the world are undergoing the same
kind of sufferings. (1 Peter 5:8-9, NIV)

The discernment and wisdom God offers us through His Word will equip us to stand against our *real* enemy—and our boss and colleagues aren't it. The devil is trying to do everything he can to keep us from God. Doesn't that make you mad? Sometimes, in order for us to move from just being blessed to being a success, we've got to get motivated, and anger is a great motivator. Now, I'm not talking about the kind of unrighteous anger between individuals that violates God's laws of love (see Matthew 22:37-39). I'm talking about spiritual resentment directed toward our spiritual enemy because you finally realize that you've been tricked most of your life by a villain who is real, sneaky, deceptive, and dangerous. That enemy has only one desire for followers of Christ: destruction!

So just how do we resist him? How do we stand firm in our faith? Peter made it perfectly clear: "Be self-controlled and alert."

When we set ourselves to be in agreement with God about what He considers good and evil, wrong and right, we are well on our way to triumph. We begin to walk in victory by first paying attention to our circumstances and our actions and then weighing what we perceive about those circumstances and actions against the truth of God's Word.

Practice this with a personal mapping exercise. When your circumstances go awry, make a note of your troubles. Examine what you have done that might have caused the problem and note those actions as well. Then, as you spend time reading the Word, ask God for the spiritual discernment and wisdom you need both to make sense of satan's efforts to foil your walk and to recognize God's desire for change. Ask God to bring your actions into alignment with His goal to make you Christlike so that you can foil satan's plans according to the Word of God. Please see the chart on the next page for an example.

I'm not saying that all problems are the result of something we have done; some are not. There is not always going to be a cause-and-effect relationship between a particular challenge at work and our behavior, but it is important to look for one. We should always question our conduct in light of Scripture's standards. If something is missing from what we should be doing, we need to go to God and repent, turn away from our transgressions, and start walking again on His path; God is faithful to forgive (see 1 John 1:8-9). In this way, even if our problem doesn't change, we can rest assured that our response to the problem meets God's expectations, not our enemy's. "Thanks be to God, who gives us the victory through our Lord Jesus Christ. Therefore, my beloved brethren, be steadfast, immovable, always abounding in the work of the Lord, knowing that your labor is not in vain in the Lord" (1 Corinthians 15:57-58). We can suck it up, celebrate even our difficulties, and watch God do His great work in the midst of our storms, confident that He will bring us through.

Problem
I seem to have lost favor with the boss. Her attitude toward me has changed. Most days she avoids speaking to me, and her behavior is obvious even to others.

Possible Related Behavior
Lately I've been secretly speaking out against her by gossiping.

Scriptural Truths
"A fool's lips bring him strife, and his mouth invites a beating. A fool's mouth is his undoing, and his lips are a snare to his soul. The words of a gossip are like choice morsels; they go down to a man's inmost parts" (Proverbs 18:6-8, NIV).

Course of Action
I will take my gripes to God rather than to my colleagues, and I will find something about her to praise in the presence of others.

Scriptural Remedy
"Let your speech always be with grace, seasoned with salt, that you may know how you ought to answer each one" (Colossians 4:6).

Unity with the Community

> Let the word of Christ dwell in you richly in all wisdom, teach-
> ing and admonishing one another in psalms and hymns and
> spiritual songs, singing with grace in your hearts to the Lord.
> (Colossians 3:16)

When we come together as Christians in the workplace, we can be a source of deep encouragement to one another. We can lift one another up in prayer with Christian affection, and we can speak encouragement and wisdom into one another's lives. *Together* we can accomplish all that the Lord desires us to achieve in any given circumstances.

But all of us who work for secular companies have been corporately conditioned to remain quiet about our faith. Have you noticed? People generally get nervous when you talk about religion, but when you talk about Christ, they get even more uncomfortable. It takes a conscious effort to unlearn the taboos of this workplace culture. But if we want to come together in Christian unity at work, we have to open ourselves up to receive another sister or brother in Christ, and sometimes it takes spiritual discernment to recognize those who are true followers of Christ.

Be advised and be very cautious. Sometimes in our excitement about our faith and our love for the Lord, we assume that anyone who says she is a Christian is in a position to give us the companionship or counsel we need (see Matthew 7:21-23). Ask the Holy Spirit to reveal to you authentic colleagues in Christ. Ask God to lead you to a close friend who can come alongside you in your walk at work. We can identify true believers. Jesus said, "By their fruits you will know them" (Matthew 7:20). So identify the fruit of a person's walk with Christ. While you're at it, ask God to help you do a quality control inspection on the fruit of your own life. Hey, none of us will ever be perfect—Lord *knows* I am so far from that—but when I asked God to reveal these things about myself, He did, warts and all! I began to see how each of us must make an effort to be spiritually better than we were yesterday. We can begin by standing on the Word today.

Standing alongside another believer you can trust is a real comfort. So ask God to guide you to another godly believer at work. If there seems to be no other Christian to connect with, find support outside the office, perhaps at church or with another Christian friend who shares your desire to bring Christ into everyday situations and who can encourage you in your efforts.

Begin to abide by the principles mentioned previously and believe that the Lord will move mightily on issues that you and your brother or sister in Christ are dealing with, either in your own lives or on behalf of people at work for whom you are interceding. Let me offer an example of how this works.

I have a treasure, a true gift from the Lord, in my friend Jestacia. Clearly God ordained for us to meet. I met her when we were both working for CNN, and although we only shared a six-month window there, that time was all we needed in order to establish a spiritually supportive friendship that is firmly rooted and grounded in Jesus Christ. Time and circumstances have moved us both out and on our own into businesses that we pray will glorify Him. As sisters in Christ, we test each other (we watch to see what fruit our businesses and lives yield), pray for each other, and stay connected to each other by telephone and through e-mail. We consistently seek "unity of the faith" (Ephesians 4:13).

- Together we stand firm in Him, having established our respective businesses on scriptural grounds and a deep abiding love to "do all to the glory of God" (1 Corinthians 10:31).
- Together we stand in Christian unity and are each other's prayer partners for personal as well as professional concerns, petitioning

the Lord on behalf of each other, bringing any issues, opportunities, or challenges to the throne of grace.

- Together we stand as lights pointing each other to Jesus, despite the miles between us (she's still in the Atlanta area, and I am in New Jersey). We aim to honor Him in all we say and do, and we hope to teach, edify, and minister daily in whatever circumstances the Lord places us.

- Together we watch, pray, connect, and agree on a consistent basis, making our requests known to God. We are witnesses to each other's ever-increasing faith, and we are able to walk more boldly and confidently as we share God's love. His peace, "which surpasses all understanding" (Philippians 4:7), undergirds us and strengthens us as we lift each other up with prayer and encouragement. We consistently offer each other business leads and professional development advice, but most important, we offer each other a hand to hold as unified members in the body of Christ. Upheld like that, we go out into the world. It is just so clear that when God is in it—God's intention is for you to win it!

God is willing to do amazing things through us in the workplace when we stand on His Word, unified with other believers, and confess our faith in His only Son. When we start yielding to the unlimited resources and power of our Almighty Father, we will begin to reap a mighty harvest for His kingdom!

Practical Application

- Commit anew to standing on the Word of God by reading it daily and acting on its instructions.
- Invite the Holy Spirit to give you wisdom and discernment as you grow in your knowledge of God's Word.

- Watch your coworkers for authentic evidence of a commitment to Christ. A changed life, not just lip service, reflects the fruit of the Spirit (see Galatians 5:22-23).
- Pray to the Father, asking Him to lead you to a prayer partner on the job.

Spiritual Truth

Therefore I also, after I heard of your faith in the Lord Jesus and your love for all the saints, do not cease to give thanks for you, making mention of you in my prayers: that the God of our Lord Jesus Christ, the Father of glory, may give to you the spirit of wisdom and revelation in the knowledge of Him, the eyes of your understanding being enlightened; that you may know what is the hope of His calling, what are the riches of the glory of His inheritance in the saints, and what is the exceeding greatness of His power toward us who believe, according to the working of His mighty power. (Ephesians 1:15-19)

The same power that raised Christ from the dead is able to bring forth everything we need for spiritual and scriptural success!

Second Steps

- Watch as well as pray (see Matthew 26:41). When we watch first, then we will know best how to pray. So watch your environment with spiritually sensitive eyes in order to secure your own steps against temptation. Then look beyond your own needs to see the needs in your office. When you see them, pray specifically, asking God to supply them.

- Connect, touch, and agree with other believers regularly on behalf of one another so that your prayers will be most effective (see Matthew 18:19).
- Create a game plan, asking the Holy Spirit for guidance on how you can best apply godly principles to your daily work in a way that will be a testimony to others of the ways of Christ.

Journal Exercises

- Keep cause-and-effect/truth-and-action charts (such as the one on page 43) whenever you encounter difficulties.
- Be honest with yourself about your own issues. Is there sin you're involved in that could be affecting your witness in the workplace? What would it take to convince you of your need to repent of that sin, to stop doing it?
- Date these entries in your journal and see if, over time, any patterns emerge. Make a note of these patterns. Then take them to God in prayer, surrendering to Him so they don't hinder what He wants to accomplish in your life.

Dare to Stand

Father God,
I am beginning to understand…
Living life by the Book is the only way to guarantee
That I'll always get Your best and not just settle for
    second place.
What I think I want
Changes like the hands of time,
Passing before me—and before I know it…

I want something else.

How fickle we can be when we're not truly at peace…

But when I do what You say, all goes according to Your plan.

When I think on my own, then I risk being out of line,

Out of sync, out of touch with Your voice,

Worse yet, missing out on Your choice.

I am beginning to understand…

That when I dare to take a stand,

When I live in right standing,

Not by my standard, but by Yours,

When I take another's hand—in Christian unity we
    each will stand…

Boldly walk!

Boldly talk!

With great faith, hope, and confidence I will let my
    light shine

In the darkest corners of this place.

You will calm the roughest seas

When I dare to stand on Thee.

That's all the backup that I need.

So let me stand and stand indeed.

Your Word, Lord, will be my lead.

In Jesus' name.

Amen.

AGREEMENT

Again I say to you that if two of you agree on earth concerning any-thing that they ask, it will be done for them by My Father in heaven. For where two or three are gathered together in My name, I am there in the midst of them.

MATTHEW 18:19-20

God is trying to get me to see that He is pleased when I come together with another believer to pray. There is strength in numbers when committed partners in Christ pull together their faith.

I thank God for the spiritual principle of agreement. Therefore, I take this step toward putting Matthew 18:19-20 into practice, knowing that when I am united in prayer with another, my God is in the midst of us. I don't have to be alone when I go to the Father. Yes, there are appropriate times to pray to Him in secret (see Matthew 6:6), but Jesus also encourages me to take the hand of another and, together, call out to God in *His* name.

Thank You, God, that corporate prayer is something I can practice here at work. I am especially honored to be in agreement with the Lord as well as with another Christian.

Action Point: Today I pray to my Father in heaven with another believer. If I cannot find someone at work to pray with, I call someone on the phone who knows the power of prayer.

EQUALITY

Our desire is not that others might be relieved while you are hard pressed, but that there might be equality. At the present time your plenty will supply what they need, so that in turn their plenty will supply what you need. Then there will be equality.

2 CORINTHIANS 8:13-14, NIV

Anyone who has worked for someone else knows that equality in the American workplace rarely exists. In general, women aren't paid the same for doing the same job that men do, and minorities with comparable experience and talent are often passed over for promotions and pay raises. But thank God that when it comes to His kingdom, there is no discrimination. When it comes to Jesus Christ, we all have an equal opportunity not just to love Him and be loved by Him, but to live for Him as well.

As a member of the body of Christ, I should make every effort to meet together with other members. Because I am uniquely designed, as they are, with particular talents and spiritual gifts, my abilities might meet their needs, and vice versa. If I'm good at writing and my sister or brother in Christ needs assistance in that area—I should offer to help. Similarly, if you are aware of an opportunity that seems perfectly suited for me, then you should communicate that information to me. If we each would seek equality by sharing the bounty of what we have and of who we are in Christ, then none of us would ever lack.

Lord, You have blessed me beyond measure (see Ephesians 1:3). Just as You commanded Abraham, whom You also blessed, let me seek to be a blessing to one of Your children (see Genesis 12:2).

Action Point: Today I offer my expertise to someone who might be able to benefit from it.

ASTROLOGY

The secret which the king has demanded, the wise men, the astrologers, the magicians, and the soothsayers cannot declare to the king. But there is a God in heaven who reveals secrets.

DANIEL 2:27-28

I know I have no business getting a cup of coffee, grabbing the newspaper, and opening up to the horoscopes every day. I know I have no business calling a 900 number from work to talk to Miss Psychic-of-the-Day to see what the stars have to say. I know I have no business going online on company time and on the company computer to "do research" about magic.

The Word of God strictly prohibits dabbling in anything that looks, smells, or sounds like the occult. And, yes, that daily horoscope is from the occult. "Take heed," Scripture says, "lest you lift your eyes to heaven, and when you see the sun, the moon, and the stars, all the host of heaven, you feel driven to worship them and serve them" (Deuteronomy 4:19).

That's the warning; now here's the blessing: "The heavens declare the glory of God; and the firmament shows His handiwork" (Psalm 19:1). God has given me His Word, His Holy Spirit, and a fellowship of believers past and present to guide me in His ways. I have no need to consult any other source of "truth." What an awesome God I have the privilege of serving! Surely His Word is enough for me.

Action Point: From today forward I take heed to look only to God as my Source of information.

BIBLE

Are you not in error because you do not know the Scriptures or the power of God?

MARK 12:24, NIV

"I just never thought I'd be one of those Bible-toting Christians."

"I'm a little afraid people will see me as a Jesus freak."

"I can hardly understand the Bible anyway, so why should I keep one at work?"

It is true that I can represent Christ to others by exhibiting good behavior. Some believe all that is necessary is that a Christian be a good person, treat others fairly, and go to church on Sundays. Although I can be a good Christian and do those good things, *I must also know the Word of God.* I will encounter spiritual fights as a believer, and if I intend to battle successfully at the office, I'd better be equipped with my sword, the Word (see Ephesians 6:17).

The Bible is a living, breathing manual for life (see Hebrews 4:12). In it are practical solutions to my personal and professional problems. I need to have it with me wherever I go, especially at work. My Bible may be the only source of strength to carry me through the day, and my Bible might just spark a conversation of eternal import along the way. The Word of God is my spiritual bread and water (see John 6:35), which I cannot live without. It contains the very power of God. That's why I need to know the Word. I need to read it, I need to speak it, and I need to hide it in my heart (see Psalm 119:11).

Action Point: If I have my Bible at work, let me take it out. If I don't have it with me, then I'll bring it in tomorrow, because in its pages I always find joy and direction to assist me in every situation.

DIVISION

I urge you, brothers, to watch out for those who cause divisions and put obstacles in your way that are contrary to the teaching you have learned. Keep away from them. For such people are not serving our Lord Christ, but their own appetites. By smooth talk and flattery they deceive the minds of naive people.

ROMANS 16:17-18, NIV

It's one thing to work in harmony with other believers, and still another to work with those who cause dissension. At my workplace I expect there to be more divisive people than coworkers committed to unity. Unfortunately, there are those who will do and say anything to counter what I have learned and believe based on the Word of God. And those divisive people are the coworkers I must make note of.

But rather than spend time and energy trying to prove my point or convert them to my way of thinking, I'm going to do what it says in the Bible. I'm going to know who they are and keep away from them! Better that I pray for them quietly than be held captive to their appetites. I cannot underestimate the potential effect their conversation might have on my conviction. I already know many of them can be persuasive with their smooth talk, even flattery. Flattery will get you nowhere? Not necessarily so. Yes, I like to hear nice things about myself, but, Lord, let me not be so easily persuaded by another who may profess Christ, but may not necessarily live to serve Him. Help me remain wise in what is good and simple concerning evil (see Matthew 10:16 and 1 Corinthians 14:20). I will keep my distance.

Action Point: Today I remove myself from situations that the Spirit tells me are dangerous.

COWORKERS

Now he who plants and he who waters are one, and each one will receive his own reward according to his own labor. For we are God's fellow workers; you are God's field, you are God's building.

1 CORINTHIANS 3:8-9

Anytime I am apt to think of myself as "just an employee" or think of others as "my" employees, the Lord reminds me that we believers are all employees of the Most High God. We are *His* workers.

So what must I do today to accomplish God's work? First, I must remember that, in the workplace, I am on equal footing with others who know and love God. Perhaps God will use me today to plant a seed of righteousness. Perhaps He will use another believer to water the seed with prayer, exhortation, or encouragement. It doesn't matter to God that, in the natural world, I may be in a supervisory position. He also doesn't mind if I am part of the rank and file. What matters to God is that I recognize one simple truth: I am called to unite with other believers to get His work done.

Lord, I am your field; let my heart be moist and open to receive direction. Let my life be fruitful, bearing green plants that yield food to feed the sheep I find here on the job. I am Your temple: Lord, let me stand firm with You as my foundation for life. Let me keep myself holy and acceptable unto You so that Your Holy Spirit will feel perfectly at home and use my life to bring glory to Your Son, Jesus Christ. I am Your laborer: Lord, let me labor in love and with joy. Let me stay committed to those You've placed in my charge. Let the work I do today speak of Your glory.

Action Point: Today I renew my commitment to accomplishing God's work as a member of heaven's team.

INJUSTICE

Do not be afraid of them. Remember the Lord, great and awesome, and fight…

NEHEMIAH 4:14

There are times when I must retreat. There are times when I must pray. And there are times when I just have to stand and fight. As Martin Luther King Jr. once said, "Injustice anywhere is a threat to justice everywhere."

In this day and age, all work environments seem wrought with difficulties. Employment decisions are not usually about what's fair; more often they're about what's cost effective. When that is the case, everyone is a potential target for trouble.

When injustice threatened his efforts to rebuild Jerusalem's walls, Nehemiah "set the people according to their families, with their swords, their spears, and their bows" (4:13). When I am faced with injustice, I thank God I have at my disposal an arsenal called "the whole armor of God" (see Ephesians 6:10-20). The most important weapon I have is the sword of the Spirit, the Word of God. This is why it's so important for me to be committed to Bible study. Because God created everything in heaven and on earth by what He said (see Genesis 1), and because Jesus stood strong against satan's temptations by always saying, "It is written…" (Matthew 4:1-11), then I must know the Word, speak the Word, and believe that the Word of God is sufficient to right any wrong. When I use the Word, I can speak to a situation and have it addressed in the spirit realm first. Then, in accordance with God's will, its effects will dissipate in the natural. The Word of God has power!

Action Point: Today as I face injustice, I turn to the Word before I react.

DISCOURAGEMENT

And He said to them, "Come aside by yourselves to a deserted place and rest a while."

MARK 6:31

Jesus' disciples suffered a major blow. They were upset and discouraged because John the Baptist had been beheaded. They went to Jesus and told Him all that had occurred, all they had just been through.

The level of compassion Jesus showed the Twelve is nothing short of amazing. John was Jesus' first cousin, and yet He didn't focus on His own grief. Instead, He encouraged His disciples to steal away. Take some time, He urged. Go, rest, and be alone.

When I suffer a major setback, I have much to gain by taking a moment to simply be still and know that God is indeed God (see Psalm 46:10). There is more comfort in this fact than in anything someone might say to make me feel better. Rest gives me an opportunity to reflect: *Maybe God wants to speak to me about a personal issue I must deal with. Maybe I've become consumed by a recent failure or a confrontation.* After rest, after reorienting myself toward God, then I am better prepared to receive encouragement from a sister or brother in Christ.

And when I'm in a position to encourage, I will sometimes do well to take my friend by the hand, find a quiet corner, and just be still with him or her, offering silent prayer, quietly asking God to have His way, softly whispering, "Peace, be still!" (Mark 4:39).

Action Point: If I am discouraged today, I seek rest in God before I seek the advice and comfort of others.

EXCELLENCE

For wisdom is a defense as money is a defense, but the excellence
of knowledge is that wisdom gives life to those who have it.

ECCLESIASTES 7:12

Isn't it interesting that the Word of God actually says that money, just like wisdom, is a defense? When I am paid at the end of the week for what should be excellent work, I use the money as a defense against poverty, against hunger; I desire to be a wise steward over my finances. Lord, as I seek excellence every day, striving to excel in every way, let me remember that it is the excellence of knowledge in the wisdom of the Lord that will ultimately sustain me. Keeping this in the front of my mind will require me to adjust the paradigm daily reinforced by the world:

• The world says wisdom comes from within, *but*…the Word says wisdom begins with fear of the Lord (see Proverbs 9:10).

• The world says knowledge is an academic degree, *but*…the Word says "knowledge of the Holy One is understanding" (Proverbs 9:10).

If I seek to uplift the work of my own hands as I toil daily, I will miss the excellence of God's work moment by moment. Is it not excellent that I awaken each morning filled with breath? Is it not excellent that the sun rises each day? Is it not excellent that I am able to open the Book of Knowledge and read a sustaining Word to get me through the day? "O LORD, our Lord, how excellent is Your name in all the earth" (Psalm 8:1).

Action Point: Today I praise God's excellence all around me in both big and small things.

INITIATIVE

And when Jesus came to the place, He looked up and saw him, and said to him, "Zacchaeus, make haste and come down, for today I must stay at your house." So he made haste and came down, and received Him joyfully.

LUKE 19:5-6

Sometimes I just have to be bold and take the initiative. That's what Jesus did when He passed through the city of Jericho, where Zacchaeus lived. Zacchaeus was a rich tax collector, considered unworthy of religious leaders' attention. Upon seeing the man, Jesus did something that no other person would because He realized that this man was interested in knowing who He was. When Zacchaeus ran ahead of the crowd and climbed a tree to catch a glimpse of the Light that was passing by, Jesus called out to him and boldly invited Himself to dinner. Our Lord took the initiative.

Because I know Jesus, others are looking at the light He reflects through me. They may not know how to speak out and begin a conversation, but I do—and I should! After all, I know, just like John the Baptist, I have been appointed a "witness of that Light" (John 1:8).

Holy Spirit, reveal to me how and when to start a conversation about God with someone who lives in the dark. Sometimes the door to another's heart will only be opened to Jesus if I obey His prompting and take the initiative to turn the knob.

Action Point: Today I pay careful attention to the voice of the Holy Spirit when I am in the presence of others.

INTIMIDATION

He had been hired to intimidate me so that I would commit a sin by doing this, and then they would give me a bad name to discredit me.

NEHEMIAH 6:13, NIV

Even back in Nehemiah's day, people attempted to rule others by intimidation. Nehemiah 6 documents the great trouble his enemies went to so he would falter in the sight of others and in the sight of God. Not much is different in today's workplace. When I set out to do a good job or when I am praised for work done well, I should not be surprised if others feel anger or jealousy and try to get me off my game:

- There are those who will do anything to keep me from doing a good job.
- They will try to get me to compromise my convictions (6:1-4).
- They will oppose me and try to slander my name (6:5-9).
- They will even resort to treachery (6:10-14).

But when God is for me, who can be against me? (see Romans 8:31). If I stand on the Word and do what I'm supposed to do, I will complete the assignment before me, and then all my enemies will have to step back and say to themselves, "Humph! God must have been the One to finish this work" (see Nehemiah 6:16).

Action Point: Today I ignore the efforts of those who try to intimidate me, remembering that my strength is from the Lord.

IGNORANCE

My people are destroyed for lack of knowledge.

HOSEA 4:6

"My people!" Not some far-off group of individuals who know nothing about the Son of the living God, but *"My people!"* Not some distant culture that has never heard the Word of God nor been exposed to the knowledge and revelation of Jesus Christ. But *"My people."*

Now, here's a frightening thought: I could actually be in church Sunday after Sunday, praising the Lord, singing hymns, and reciting psalms. I could pray morning and evening and still be destroyed. I can be confident I am saved but go no further to know my Lord. Furthermore, I can be saved and still experience daily defeat because of my ignorance not just of God's Word but also of the wiles of the enemy.

Once I confess Jesus as my Lord and Savior and set my heart on living righteously *before* Him, I am given authority *in* Him. Jesus said, "Behold, I give you the authority to trample on serpents and scorpions, and over all the power of the enemy, and nothing shall by any means hurt you" (Luke 10:19). Why do I need such authority? Because if I don't seek to *know Jesus personally*—if I remain content simply knowing what it takes to be saved and little else—then I can be hurt, torn down, beat up, bopped around, and ultimately "destroyed" because I didn't take the time to get a spiritual education.

Lord, teach me what I need to know so that illumination will overpower my ignorance. "Let your heart retain my words; keep my commands, and live. Get wisdom! Get understanding!" (Proverbs 4:4-5).

Action Point: Today I ask God to begin revealing Himself to me as I have never experienced before.

"STEAL AWAY"

So He Himself often withdrew into the wilderness and prayed.

LUKE 5:16

At times I feel all alone. At times I feel as if the Christian walk is a lonely walk.

Even though I'm blessed with godly friends who love me, support me, and, most important, pray for me, in certain moments I feel as if it's just me and the Lord. *Just us.*

I often try to compensate for the quiet by losing myself in my work or surrounding myself with people. But when I feel truly lonely, that deeper need can only be fulfilled if I steal away to pray. Jesus made a habit of this, and He is the divine example of how to walk this life of faith successfully. There's always so much to do, and finding the time to be alone with the Lord may seem nearly impossible. But it is essential.

"To everything there is a season.... He has made everything beautiful in its time" (Ecclesiastes 3:1,11). Even times of loneliness can be beautiful if I would simply honor the season I find myself in and press closer into the arms of my heavenly Father. He knows all about my troubles. He knows the aching of my heart. He knows the secret places of pain that need to be made whole.

I can find wholeness only in Him, because, when all else passes away, it really is just the two of us. So, Lord, help me to make private time with You a priority. That time will make all the difference in my world.

Action Point: Today I set aside and protect a designated time for the Lord.

LOSING IT

Therefore humble yourselves under the mighty hand of God, that He may exalt you in due time, casting all your care upon Him, for He cares for you.

1 PETER 5:6-7

Some days it takes every ounce of patience I have to do with grace all that I must get done. "Lord, help me keep it together!" I cry. In these difficult moments I must give my circumstances completely over to Him or risk "losing it" (not a pretty sight). I must humble myself before God's mighty and quite capable hands and just breathe...

In times like these, I do well to go to my prayer partner for support. After all, God loves me and has invited me—one who labors and is heavy laden—to come to Him, for His yoke is easy and His burden is light. In the very bosom of Jesus Christ I can find rest, and at His feet I must leave my cares (see Matthew 11:28-30).

Today I don't have to lose it! Not today, not tomorrow, and not ever, as long as I remember to bring all my baggage to God. He can handle what I cannot. If He can hold up the sun and the moon, hang the countless stars in the heavens, and keep the world spinning in place, He can handle a little anxiety from me every once in a while. And then, in His power, I'll be able to handle it too.

Action Point: Today I go to God in prayer at the first sign of personal or professional overload!

LOOSING IT!

Whatever you bind on earth will be bound in heaven, and whatever you loose on earth will be loosed in heaven.

MATTHEW 18:18

Losing it is very different from *"Loosing it!"* And there's a B-I-G difference in how I get control over the two. The Lord knew that I would find myself in situations that require on-the-spot, take-charge kind of power. Thank God for Jesus! When He went to the cross, He destroyed the works of the enemy. That means that as a true follower of Christ (and as long as the devil isn't at work in me) I can take authority over all the works of the devil and keep him at bay.

What exactly does Jesus mean when He says "whatever you bind on earth" in Matthew 18:18? Jesus teaches that there are spiritual forces, dark forces, at work around me. I can get the upper hand on these situations if I take my authority over them. Jesus also reveals that there are good forces filled with the Light of the Lord that I can call upon to work on my behalf if I simply speak God's Word to the situation.

So when I notice certain things around me that I know are not from God, traits like envy, revenge, jealousy, anger, and control, I can bind those things in Jesus' name, and God promises they will be bound in heaven. Similarly, I can *loose* the Christlike qualities that I know will help ease circumstances around me—qualities like cooperation, patience, love, kindness, and self-control (see Galatians 5:22-23). Today, in faith, I will do as Jesus instructed. When I need to get a handle on things, I will bind the hand of the enemy and *loose* the love of the Lord.

Action Point: Today I learn to exercise the authority God has given me to thwart the plans of the enemy.

Persecution

*What persecutions I endured. And out of them all the Lord deliv-
ered me. Yes, and all who desire to live godly in Christ Jesus will
suffer persecution.*

2 Timothy 3:11-12

The apostle Paul is a hero to all who attempt to live for Jesus Christ.
And he tells it just like it is. No sugarcoating. He makes it plain what I
may endure, but he also gives me great hope: No matter what I'm going
through, my God will deliver me from it all!

When I set my heart on getting my spiritual act together so that I
can effectively be in the world but not of it (see John 17:14-18), persecution *will*—not might—be a part of my life. Sometimes that persecution will originate in the workplace. The best way to endure persecution
is to make sure I am *prayed up, buckled up, and charged up* to fight:

- I get *prayed up* by bringing God into every aspect of my life.
  Prayer doesn't always have to be an on-my-knees thing. It can
  simply be a "Help, Lord!" at my desk.
- I get *buckled up* by literally, verbally, and daily putting on the
  whole armor of God (see Ephesians 6:10-20).
- I get *charged up* by equipping myself with the Word of God
  so I am ready to face any situation. People may have their evil
  intentions, but the devil is behind them. When persecuted, I
  have to rely on God's Word and His promise to bring me
  through any difficult situation. All I have to do is stand. God
  will do the rest. *My God will deliver me from it all!*

Action Point: Today I do what is required to get prayed up, buckled
up, and charged up!

STRENGTH

Though one may be overpowered by another, two can withstand him. And a threefold cord is not quickly broken.

ECCLESIASTES 4:12

Without some form of Christian unity at work, I will succumb to the pressures of the daily grind. It is easier for the enemy to overtake me with doubt, fear, and spiritual filth when I am in the battle alone, and trying to stand for Jesus in the midst of the corporate mind-set *is* a battle.

Father, please provide someone—perhaps even more than one—with whom I can stand so that we will not feel overpowered or be over-run. Your Word says two are better than one and three is even stronger. If I fall, I will be lifted up. My believing friends will help to keep me centered, and they will help defend me when I might otherwise be over-powered (see Ecclesiastes 4:9-12).

When we stick together as a band of brothers, we can use our authority in Jesus Christ to bind the hand of the enemy and cancel his evil delights (see Matthew 18:18). By faith and faith alone, we will together withstand "the wiles of the devil" (Ephesians 6:11). Together, equipped with the whole armor of God, we will take our walk with You to a new level.

Action Point: Today I turn my heart toward a Christian friend whom I can encourage and strengthen, knowing that I will also be strengthened in the process.

SWORD

For the word of God is living and powerful, and sharper than any two-edged sword, piercing even to the division of soul and spirit, and of joints and marrow, and is a discerner of the thoughts and intents of the heart.

HEBREWS 4:12

The Word of God describes its own power as being sharper than any two-edged sword. If I were going into battle, would I forget the one thing that is going to protect me? The weapon that is going to allow me to fight my way out and back to safety? Absolutely not!

Well, that's what it's like every day when I go to work without spending time in God's Word. Some mornings (and, oftentimes, many evenings) I find myself either too rushed or too tired to simply take that moment and be with the Lord. Yet I know that spending time studying the Word of God is essential if I'm going to sustain a high level of success in my walk at work. The office is one of the most important places in which I need to be able to defend myself and guard my spirit.

Lord, help me to internalize the knowledge that Your Word brings life and that You want to use it to shine a light on my intentions, my actions, and my attitudes. When I wield the Sword of the Spirit, which is the Word of God, then I can accurately discern the thoughts and intentions of my heart with Your perspective and not mine.

Action Point: This week I commit Hebrews 4:12 to memory. This is a sure way to sharpen my sword.

TEMPTATION

God is faithful, who will not allow you to be tempted beyond what you are able, but with the temptation will also make the way of escape, that you may be able to bear it.

1 CORINTHIANS 10:13

The way to escape temptation, the first step toward safety, is always obedience to God, and obedience comes only by knowing God. Do I feed my spirit knowledge the way I feed my flesh food? Whatever I feed the most is what will grow, and a starved spirit will not have the strength to resist temptation. God warns us repeatedly of the serious, *serious* consequences of ignorance: "Because you have rejected knowledge, I also will reject you from being priest for Me; because you have forgotten the law of your God, I also will forget your children" (Hosea 4:6).

Fighting temptation, especially at the workplace, can be very difficult. We develop close-knit working relationships and, in some cases, spend more time with colleagues than we do with our mates and families. We often fear the loss of our reputations or a missed promotion more than we fear disappointing God. The best way to fight temptation is by reading the Word of God and by seeing temptation's attraction through our spiritual eyes. If temptation showed up with a red suit, horns, and a tail, we would never get close enough to be burned.

Action Point: Today I remember that if the Word of God doesn't say yes, my answer must be no.

UNITY

Jesus answered him, "The first of all the commandments is: 'Hear, O Israel, the LORD our God, the LORD is one. And you shall love the LORD your God with all your heart, with all your soul, with all your mind, and with all your strength.' This is the first commandment. And the second, like it, is this: 'You shall love your neighbor as yourself.' There is no other commandment greater than these."

MARK 12:29-31

Bringing unity to the body of Christ is uppermost on the mind of God. For God Himself is an example of divine unity: One in Three, Three in One, the Father, the Son, and the Holy Spirit coexisting perfectly in love.

> When I look at the example of the Trinity,
> I see nothing less than divinity.
> God, my Father, forever draw me near.
> Jesus, thank You for Your saving grace.
> Holy Spirit, have Your way,
> Abiding in me every day.

Let me use this book "for the equipping of the saints for the work of ministry, for the edifying of the body of Christ, till we all come to the unity of the faith and of the knowledge of the Son of God, to a perfect man, to the measure of the stature of the fullness of Christ" (Ephesians 4:12-13). May "the grace of the Lord Jesus Christ, and the love of God, and the communion of the Holy Spirit be with [us] all. Amen" (2 Corinthians 13:14).

Action Point: Today I consciously act to love my neighbor so that we can work in harmony and live in unity.

CHANGE Yourself and Your Conversation

Walk in wisdom toward those who are outside, redeeming the time.
Let your conversation be always full of grace, seasoned with salt, so
that you may know how to answer everyone.

Colossians 4:5 (NKJV) and 4:6 (NIV)

Question: When God was busy creating *all* that is created—the sun, the moon, the stars, humankind—why didn't He first dig in His heavenly closet and pull out His Super-Duper Creation Kit?

Answer: He didn't have to. He simply spoke the Word: "Then God said, 'Let there be light'" (Genesis 1:3).

Now, it can be difficult to comprehend God's omnipotence, but I'm going to help you by presenting a series of equations that I want you to ponder until you get it—and I mean really get it! In fact, I want you to do this as an oral exercise. Somehow, when we say things aloud, their meanings sink in. You won't need a pen and paper or a calculator. The only thing you will need are your spiritual eyes. The equations are so simple, yet millions have missed their significance. I missed it for most of my life! I want to make sure you don't miss it (see chart on next page).

It is so important to watch the words we speak and equally important to watch the words we believe. You know, we're the ones who complicate this God thing! Jesus has made it so simple for us, if only we would just trust Him and do what He says. When we obey His commands and, by faith, believe His Word, what was hidden is revealed and what was in darkness comes into the light.

The next step of our S.U.C.C.E.S.S. walk is to extend our obedience to include how we communicate with others.

Again, a new commandment I write to you, which thing is true in Him and in you, because the darkness is passing away, and the true light is already shining. He who says he is in the light, and hates his brother, is in darkness until now. He who loves his brother abides in the light, and there is no cause for stumbling in him. But he who hates his brother is in darkness and walks in darkness, and does not know where he is going, because the darkness has blinded his eyes. (1 John 2:8-11)

With that as our commandment, our conversation should be all about truth, not lies; grace, not condemnation; light, not darkness.

Repent therefore of this your wickedness, and pray God if perhaps the thought of your heart may be forgiven you. (Acts 8:22)

Bread	=	Jesus *(John 6:35)*
Light	=	Jesus *(John 1:6-9)*
Life	=	Jesus *(John 14:6)*
Truth	=	Jesus *(John 14:6)*
The Way	=	Jesus *(John 14:6)*
The Word	=	Jesus *(John 1:14)*
Therefore, our words should	:	bring sustenance, shine a light, foster life, speak truth, and point the way to the Word, which is Jesus.

Repentance is a word that makes us all feel as if we've done something wrong, said something wrong, or walked in a way that we shouldn't have. And that is indeed the truth of the matter. Before we can consistently speak in a manner befitting our faith, we must change! "Change?" you say. Yes. We must turn away from anything that hurts the heart of God. We want success; we want favor with our Lord; we want all the blessings He is so gracious to give. But, as my mentor Sister Marsha says, "We don't want to obey." We can talk all we want about being spiritual and in the light. We can pray until we are hoarse from hollering to heaven, but unless we truly experience godly sorrow over our sin, we will experience only half-successes that lead to full-frustrations with a God we think doesn't answer our prayers. "What's He waiting for?" we ask. He is waiting for us to choose change.

> For godly sorrow produces repentance leading to salvation, not
> to be regretted; but the sorrow of the world produces death.
> (2 Corinthians 7:10)

If we want life, then let us fully understand this is the crucial requirement of repentance. We can try over and over again to speak well of others, to watch our words, and to be faithful to God, but if we don't begin that journey with real sorrow for how we've walked in the past, we will fail. It is our repentance, our confession of faith, and the shed blood of Jesus Christ (see Revelation 12:11) that give us the victory.

COMPASSIONATE CONVERSATION

> Death and life are in the power of the tongue,
> And those who love it will eat its fruit.
> (Proverbs 18:21)

Godly compassion means caring more about someone's soul than you do about anything that person can do for you. Therefore, compassion must become a key element in our everyday exchanges with others.

Believe it or not, every man or woman whom you and I encounter at work, even the person whom we just can't take for another second, is loved equally by our Father. If that person is a non-Christian, he or she is a potential brother or sister in Christ. (If that person is a Christian, he or she *is* already our brother or sister!) God doesn't want to lose any one of His children (see Matthew 18:14); therefore, our conversation must always be seasoned with salt and grace in order to let others see the hope of Christ shining through our lives. If the love of Christ has changed us, then that same love can transform others.

Jesus expressed this hope in the story of the woman who'd lost her coins. "What woman, having ten silver coins, if she loses one coin, does not light a lamp, sweep the house, and search carefully until she finds it? And when she has found it, she calls her friends and neighbors together, saying, 'Rejoice with me, for I have found the piece which I lost!' Likewise, I say to you, there is joy in the presence of the angels of God over one sinner who repents" (Luke 15:8-10).

When we encounter people who are lost, we should hope that they will be intrigued by *our* love for Christ and that our love will spur their desire to know Him better. Think about the people you just adore being around. Why do you like them so much? Maybe they always seem to be joyful, or they always have a word of encouragement. Maybe they always look forward rather than backward. Maybe you admire their peace and calm. Those are the kinds of people others seek to emulate. As you seek God, stand on His Word, and learn to love and obey Him, people will become attracted to the Light within you. You may never have said anything to them about who Jesus Christ is, but the spiritual fruit on the plate of your life makes them want to "taste and see that the LORD is good" (Psalm 34:8). So when you do communicate with them, feed them with the words of truth the way Jesus did.

> Now Jesus called His disciples to Himself and said, "I have
> compassion on the multitude, because they have now continued
> with Me three days and have nothing to eat. And I do not
> want to send them away hungry, lest they faint on the way."
> (Matthew 15:32)

What a revelation! Reading this speaks to my spirit on so many different levels. Although Jesus was speaking of the crowd's physical need, think about the spiritual implications!

- Jesus calls Himself the bread of life, reminding us that if we go to Him we will never go hungry (see John 6:35). The crowd had gone to Him, just as we must go to Him.
- Jesus has such great compassion for the multitude, as He does still for all of us today, that when we "continue on" with Him, He will never send us away hungry. He promises to feed us.
- Jesus knew then, as He knows now, that if He is not the One to feed us, we will "faint on the way."

According to Christ's example, our compassion for others should be reflected in the way we communicate with them and treat them.

PRACTICING THE LOST ARTS OF COMPASSION, COURTESY, AND GRACE

> Finally, all of you be of one mind, having compassion for one
> another, love as brothers, be tenderhearted, be courteous; not
> returning evil for evil or reviling for reviling, but on the contrary

blessing, knowing that you were called to this, that you may
inherit a blessing. (1 Peter 3:8-9)

To be tenderhearted simply means to extend kindness—and that's sure
an underrated personal attribute in this day and age! What exactly does
kindness look like? Well, it has many expressions that all reflect the face
of Christ because Jesus Christ Himself is our best example of tenderness, kindness, and mercy. How can we show others a tender heart?
Here are a few suggestions.

- Grab a cup of coffee for someone else in the office when you're
  out getting yours.
- Instead of throwing away your morning paper on the commute
  in, offer it to the passenger sitting next to you.
- Pay for lunch for a coworker who is in the cafeteria line behind
  you…just because.
- Pick up flowers for the cleaning woman at the office to say
  thanks because she has a thankless job.
- Help lift a harried coworker's load even if you are busy. Extend
  yourself just a little with the sincere and simple question "How
  can I help?"—and then help!

Being tenderhearted is a lovely way to let the light of Christ shine
from you and bless others. So ask God to give you a tender heart, love,
and compassion for your coworkers. After all, He shows you endless
compassion every day. Let's open our eyes and hearts by tuning in to
another person's frequency for a change, doing whatever we can to
eliminate the static and be clear in our communication, intentions,
and support.

Grace is a gift that God freely gives us; we should in turn offer grace
to others. When we extend gracious acts to someone else, we bring joy to

the heart of God and are sometimes blessed in return. I can't tell you how many times I've been extended a discount on a purchase based on a coupon I didn't have, been upgraded to first class on a plane because the ticket agent felt bad after I had waited patiently in line, or received flowers from near strangers for whom I've done professional favors without charging. God bestows favor on those who extend favor to His children.

Common courtesy can take you a looooong way. I know this is going to sound basic, but whatever happened to "please" and "thank you"? My friend Mary says that "excuse me" works well too. When you're in the middle of talking to someone and a coworker butts in with a need, take the high road through silent prayer. At some point or another, we all can be accused of being rude. Sometimes we become so consumed with our issues that we forget our manners. Besides, don't you take notice when someone asks for something and attaches a "thank you" or "when you get the chance" or "I really appreciate it"? Aren't you more willing to make it happen for them? It is amazing how our words and demeanor can defuse a situation. When we speak God into our circumstances, He awakens justice in the spiritual realm. Our conversation then opens up the pathway leading to Christ, who can change any confrontation. When we choose to change, through true repentance, God is pleased and angels rejoice. When we extend compassionate grace through our actions and our words, God comes to our rescue daily.

Practical Application

This month commit to extending the art of courtesy to your colleagues and supervisors. See what happens. You will not get a reaction from everyone because a lot of people are just too self-absorbed to pay attention, but your thoughtfulness will be appreciated by those who are still sensitive enough to notice. Would you *please* try it today? Listen, *I really appreciate it.*

Spiritual Truth

For the word of God is living and powerful, and sharper than any two-edged sword, piercing even to the division of soul and spirit, and of joints and marrow, and is a discerner of the thoughts and intents of the heart. (Hebrews 4:12)

The Word of God shines a light on the life and death contained in our own words.

Third Steps

- As you practice the art of courtesy, think, *What would Jesus do?* Whether you are a banker or baseball player, a maître d' or mom, God wants you to consider His will and agenda at every crossroad and be considerate to others who are traveling beside you.
- Learn to listen for the voice of the Lord. He is at work in your current environment. Ask the Holy Spirit to reveal to you opportunities in which you can "let your light so shine before men, that they may see your good works and glorify your Father in heaven" (Matthew 5:16). The Holy Spirit loves it when God gets all the credit!
- Actively involve yourself in prayer, praise, and worship of the Lord on behalf of others at work, especially those who don't know the Lord. God honors the righteous prayers of those who earnestly intercede for His children (see James 5:16).

Journal Exercises

Begin to keep a record of prayer requests for coworkers and notes on how you can extend to them tenderness, grace, and compassion. Don't forget praise reports, so that when the need is met or the situation is resolved, God will always get the glory.

Also make a note of kindnesses that others extend to you. These reminders will both foster an attitude of gratefulness in your heart and provide ideas about gestures you can extend to others.

The Word of God

Sharper than any two-edged sword, more powerful than
    the forces of hell,
Your Word.
Today I purpose in my heart to speak the Truth, know-
    ing that all else eventually fails.
Because the truth of the matter is that without Your
    Word,
I am lost.
A sheep without a Shepherd.
A laborer without a heavenly Boss.
Some days I act as if that really wouldn't be so bad,
Except I understand the cost.
When I am not yielding to You, Lord, I become disori-
    ented...confused...lost.
What separates the wheat from the tare? The wheat
    stands in Your field.
Stands tall. Stands on Your Word. Stands ready to do
    Your will.

The wheat is able to bend and not break when the
weather changes.

And the weather changes at work moment by moment.

But when I stand on Your words of Truth, I can confidently say:

I'm not shaken by the storms.

I know that because I am a Christian I'm different from
all the rest.

Not better—not boasting—just clear that with You,
I can be my best.

My peace is because of Jesus Christ,

Who is cleaning me up and changing my life.

Therefore I'm not restricted by the world,

Just open to the endless possibilities of You.

So, Lord, I'm standing on Your Word today.

In the name of Jesus, this I pray.

Amen.

ACCOUNTABILITY

For our boasting is this: the testimony of our conscience that we conducted ourselves in the world in simplicity and godly sincerity, not with fleshly wisdom but by the grace of God, and more abundantly toward you.

2 CORINTHIANS 1:12

Every day I should ask myself, *Who's watching me? Who is listening to how I speak to others? Who is looking at my behavior and assessing my Christian character?*

The truth is, while others observe me, it is the Holy Spirit who stands and observes all my actions, because He is the One living inside me. No wonder God knows my every thought! His Spirit resides within the temple of my body—and it is miraculous that He *chooses* to dwell with me. With all my frailties and faults, all my backsliding and impure thoughts, He still abides with me! Thank You, God!

Lord, hold me accountable to You. Teach me how to sift all that I think and do through the love filters of Christ. Lord, let me boast not in my achievements, but in what You've been able to do through me. Let me express genuine concern toward others, extending Your grace to them because daily You extend Yours to me.

Lord, I am your laborer. When I speak love, patience, and peace to others, I allow You to speak through me. Teach me to measure my words, Lord, for You will hold me accountable for every utterance that I speak (see Matthew 12:36-37). Let me love others with godly sincerity, extending to them an overabundance of grace.

Action Point: Today I pay careful attention to my words, lest any of them dishonor the Holy Spirit.

APPRECIATION

Through Jesus, therefore, let us continually offer to God a sacrifice of praise—the fruit of lips that confess his name. And do not forget to do good and to share with others, for with such sacrifices God is pleased.

HEBREWS 13:15-16, NIV

Isn't it strange that the world, with a cynical tone, calls someone who is always ready to help a do-gooder? God's Word, however, specifically commands us to remember others and to be *good* to them, even to *share* with them! God smiles from heaven when He sees His children extending loving-kindness to one another.

Even more important than doing good to others is praising God for His goodness, and not just once a week, for one day is not sufficient to thank Him for all His gifts. No, Scripture admonishes me to *continually* offer God praise. In fact, the Bible calls that offering a sacrifice.

When I praise God for what I could never repay Him, it's a sacrifice in which I freely give all of my appreciation to Him. He is good, merciful, protective, gentle, healing, wise, warm. There is power in His breath, His touch, His Word, His Son, His guidance, His Holy Spirit. I praise Him for His love, His holiness, His standard, His truth, His angels, His actions, and His almighty never-ending grace! When I continually offer my praise to Him, I show Him my appreciation for everyday miracles. When I share with others what He has done for me, I give them something that will help them be successful in their walk with Christ. For we are made victorious by the blood of the Lamb and the word of our testimony (see Revelation 12:11).

Action Point: Today I offer God a sacrifice of praise continually throughout the day.

BEHAVIOR

But as for you, speak the things which are proper for sound doctrine: that the older men be sober, reverent, temperate, sound in faith, in love, in patience; the older women likewise, that they be reverent in behavior, not slanderers, not given to much wine, teachers of good things.

TITUS 2:1-3

In order to be successful in my walk with Christ and in my walk at work, I want to aim high when it comes to my character and my conduct. That's what having a good reputation is all about. How can I get that good reputation? By consistently doing the good things of God and rejecting the sinful things of self. By vigilantly monitoring my own intentions, thoughts, and actions toward others. By examining what I think, not just what I say and do.

The key to success is knowing the Word of God, so that when I speak, I speak God's Truth. My doctrine should accurately reflect the truth of who God is and what He has to say about any situation. For, truly, there is a word written for all occasions in this instruction manual called the Holy Bible. Some people just open their mouths and throw out a scripture that seems appropriate without considering the context in which that word was given. In my approach to the Word, however, I want to be sober-minded and clearheaded so that when I speak, I speak God's Truth. Patient, levelheaded, faithful, loving—these are characteristics of behavior befitting a Christian (see also Titus 1:8-9). When others observe me, I hope they will see these qualities in me.

Action Point: Today I ask God to reveal to me a truth in His Word that I've never understood before.

CHARACTER

Do not be misled: "Bad company corrupts good character." Come back to your senses as you ought, and stop sinning; for there are some who are ignorant of God—I say this to your shame.

1 CORINTHIANS 15:33-34, NIV

Yes, character still counts! God says so, and I should strive for godly character, not just in my personal relationships, but in my professional ones as well. I should ask this question when I think of those with whom I associate: Has God placed them in my life so that I can minister to them (offer support, encouragement, or a Christlike example), or has God placed them in my life so that together we can enjoy fellowship?

Let me think about the crowd with whom Christ spent time. They were a fairly motley group. He was seen with tax collectors, sinners, and the like, but His intention on this earth was not to have a good time. His intention was to minister grace and salvation.

Lord, let me not become a theological snob with a holier-than-thou attitude, staying away from those who don't know You. Rather, let me discern Your purposes for my interactions with others based on this guideline from 1 Corinthians 15:33: If I find myself mingling with those of questionable character, whether deal makers or deadbeats, help me to guard against the possibility of going astray. When we exchange words, let those words plant in them seeds for Christ. For I know: One plants and one waters, but it is You "who gives the increase" (1 Corinthians 3:6-8). May my character choices be godly choices.

Action Point: Today as I make the acquaintance of a colleague or associate, I ask God to reveal to me the kind of relationship He has in mind for us.

COMMUNICATION

Let no corrupt communication proceed out of your mouth, but that which is good to the use of edifying, that it may minister grace unto the hearers.

EPHESIANS 4:29, KJV

My communication is more than the sum of my conversations. I may communicate verbally or nonverbally, but when I do use words, let me be honest. Let me be authentic, not smiling one minute and seething the next. Let the words of my heart be pure and true. When I lift up the name of the Lord Jesus Christ, prompt me to be mindful of how I speak to others. I want my words to please You.

I want my words to be consistent with my walk. I never want someone to say of me, "Well, she's *basically* a good person, but…" For it is better that I live righteously than straddle the fence. Let me be either hot or cold in the confession of my faith, because that in-between—that lukewarm spot—gets me nothing. While it does sound harsh, God says to the lukewarm, "I will vomit you out of My mouth" (Revelation 3:16).

Help me, O God, to watch what I say. When I open my mouth, let my communication be pleasing, suitable for edification and for building up, not tearing down. And Holy Spirit, teach me to discern when I should keep silent and pray quietly. I don't always need to say something aloud, because no matter what or when, I can say it to God.

My communication should minister to all who hear. My words should be a soothing salve to all, seasoned with grace and love, softly nurturing and embracing those in need of comfort.

Action Point: Today I invite my prayer partner to hold me accountable and bring any ungodly speech to my attention.

SARCASM

Then [the pharaoh] said to them, "The LORD had better be with you when I let you and your little ones go! Beware, for evil is ahead of you."

EXODUS 10:10

Why is sarcasm so common in the workplace? It bites, it belittles, and it bewilders even the bravest of hearts, especially when someone in authority practices it. Sarcasm, especially when it's used to put anyone "in his place," cuts like a knife. It is a common method of control that reveals the worst of the human heart.

With his hardened heart, Pharaoh used sarcasm to try to undermine the confidence and mission of Moses, who demanded that he let God's people go. Moses and his protégé/brother, Aaron, came to warn Pharaoh that God was going to send a plague of locusts to Egypt. Yet there he stood, refusing to humble himself before God, trying desperately to turn the tide of justice that was coming in against him.

People are going to be sarcastic. Even I can appreciate the humor that puts things in perspective, but I must not forget that sarcasm wounds. I remember the times when it has hurt me. Lord, when I am tempted to be sarcastic, remind me that "a word fitly spoken is like apples of gold in settings of silver" (Proverbs 25:11). Help me be aware that You are my God, who can give me strength to hold my tongue. Help me exercise that strength with others by not using cheap tactics to put someone else down. Instead, use me to lift them up and point the way to You.

Action Point: Today I intentionally avoid sarcasm and examine the difference this action has on my communications with others.

DISCRETION

> *Then they said to one another, "Look, this dreamer is coming!*
> *Come therefore, let us now kill him and cast him into some pit;*
> *and we shall say, 'Some wild beast has devoured him.' We shall see*
> *what becomes of his dreams!"*
>
> GENESIS 37:19-20

Joseph dreamed big dreams. Why? Because the Lord had big plans for him. God revealed to Joseph in a dream that he would become highly esteemed. There's a vision I wouldn't mind having, a vision I would probably run to share with those closest to my heart.

When Joseph told his family of his dream, however, he started a fire that nearly cost him his life. It's easy to blame the wicked brothers for all of Joseph's misfortune, but other factors were also at work:

- First, Joseph really should have kept his mouth shut. *Sometimes the Lord has a word for me that should not be shared with others right away.*
- Second, Joseph must have sensed he was his father Jacob's favorite child. He didn't exactly downplay the benefits. Like-wise, in the workplace, some people will never be happy about the good works God is doing in your life. *When God gives me favor on the job, I don't need to go blabbing all about it.*
- Third, Joseph's prideful brothers suffered from feelings of in-feriority. *When I see the good work God is doing in someone else's life, I will be happy for that person and will lift him or her up in prayer.* Remember that pride and pettiness are perfect friends.

Action Point: Today I exercise discernment about what I share with others regarding the work of God in my life.

PREJUDICE

Joseph ate by himself, and his brothers were served at a separate table. The Egyptians sat at their own table because Egyptians despise Hebrews and refuse to eat with them.

GENESIS 43:32, NLT

The prejudice in Joseph's day was just as real, painful, and destructive as it is today. Joseph suffered many hardships because of the prejudice his brothers held against him and later because of the Egyptians' prejudice against him, but nevertheless his dream came true.

Joseph was the only man in the land who could correctly interpret a dream for Pharaoh. His interpretation, as with his earlier dreams back home in Israel, was from the Lord. Pharaoh recognized Joseph's authentic connection to the one, true, living God and was moved by God to exalt young Joseph.

In Genesis 43, Joseph eats alone not because he is a Jew, but because he is serving in a position like a king. His brothers sit apart due to the Egyptians' prejudice against the Jewish people, but because of Joseph's faithfulness to God, that injustice wouldn't last long either.

The Hebrew boy—once nearly left for dead in a well, sold into slavery, thrown into prison, and then moved by the Lord into a position of great power—overcame his life trials. Because he never forgot God, Joseph was able to push beyond prejudice and into prestige. Not only that, but the grace of God enabled him to extend similar grace and favor to his entire family (Genesis 45:3-20). "Where sin abounded, grace did much more abound" (Romans 5:20, KJV). Lord, teach me grace.

Action Point: Today I ask God to reveal any prejudice that lives in my heart so that He can begin the work of replacing it with His grace.

EMOTION

And being in agony, He prayed more earnestly. Then His sweat became like great drops of blood falling down to the ground. When He rose up from prayer, and had come to His disciples, He found them sleeping from sorrow. Then He said to them, "Why do you sleep? Rise and pray, lest you enter into temptation."

LUKE 22:44-46

When my Lord prayed to the Father in His eleventh hour, He cried out, "Father, if it is Your will, take this cup away from Me; nevertheless not My will, but Yours, be done" (Luke 22:42). Rising from prayer, Jesus must have felt deep despair, knowing that the very moment for which He had come to earth was at hand. He went to His disciples for support only to find them asleep on the job. All He had asked of them was to stay awake and pray, but overwhelmed with their own sorrow and exhaustion, they failed to be there for Jesus in His time of need.

When I am overcome by my feelings, I can choose to give in to my emotions and become self-absorbed. Or while honoring those feelings, I can still make choices that enable me to remain present and available to those I love.

When I am filled with emotion and heavy of heart, Lord, strengthen me, so that I don't give in to my emotional state. Instead, equip me to do what Jesus did. If I need to cry, then I will cry. If I need to steal away, then I will find a quiet place to become renewed. And here on the job, when my emotions are poised to get the very best of me, I will seek refuge in only one place: I will seek to find my rest in You.

Action Point: In the face of sorrow, I take Jesus' advice and pray lest I "enter into temptation."

RISK

*Then the daughter of Pharaoh came down to bathe at the river. And
her maidens walked along the riverside; and when she saw the ark
among the reeds, she sent her maid to get it. And when she opened it,
she saw the child, and behold, the baby wept. So she had compassion
on him, and said, "This is one of the Hebrews' children."*

EXODUS 2:5-6

One act of kindness, an outpouring of true compassion, can change the
course of history. The daughter of Pharaoh showed compassion for baby
Moses, and decades later God used Moses to help free the Israelites from
bondage and slavery. She took a great risk in saving Moses' life, considering that her father had ordered the execution of Hebrew infants.

Compassion is a cornerstone of the Christian faith, and Jesus doesn't
expect me to limit my sensitivities once I get to work. Many people
believe that compassion has no place on the job. For this reason, compassion is a risky attribute. People mistake it for weakness, a mistake of
great import.

But Jesus didn't worry about what others would think: "Now a
leper came to Him, imploring Him, kneeling down to Him and saying
to Him, 'If You are willing, You can make me clean.' Then Jesus, moved
with compassion, stretched out His hand and touched him, and said to
him, 'I am willing; be cleansed'" (Mark 1:40-41).

God can use my compassion to win others to Christ. Only He has
the power to cleanse, but by His grace and moved with compassion, I
have the power to change the course of history for those I meet.

Action Point: Today I risk extending compassion to someone who
may not return it, knowing that my reward comes from God.

FORGIVENESS

Bear with each other and forgive whatever grievances you may have against one another. Forgive as the Lord forgave you.

COLOSSIANS 3:13, NIV

Lord, is there anyone at work against whom I am harboring anger? I know that a tenet of my Christian faith is forgiving others and not harboring any hate. Yet somehow at work it is easy to hold on to contempt, calling it innocuous *office politics,* a phrase that seems to render me innocent of sinfulness.

But, Lord, I know You don't think that way. You say that if I have anything against a brother or sister, I must leave Your presence and get my business straight before You will accept my offerings (see Matthew 5:23-24). So, Father, You know this is going to be hard. I don't want to expose myself. I don't want to feel anyone's disregard. But that's not the point; that's not Your greatest concern. So I will take a deep breath, submit myself in prayer, and ask You to prepare the heart of that other person. Then I know You will lead the way to our reconciliation.

Holy Spirit, I know what I must do. Father God, I will "be reconciled to [my] brother" out of love for You (Matthew 5:24). Jesus, I hear Your voice saying, *Forgive and ask forgiveness for yourself, too.* I can't remain in Your presence, Lord, when I still have this thing left to do. Therefore, Lord, open up an opportunity; crack the door or perhaps a window. Obedience is far better than sacrifice (see 1 Samuel 15:22); I know that's what Your Word proves. So I am ready to confront and forgive; help me, Lord, and I will do it.

Action Point: Today I seize whatever opportunity God sets before me to bridge the gap of unforgiveness between me and a colleague.

FRIENDSHIP

*Do you not know that friendship with the world is hostility toward
God? Therefore whoever wishes to be a friend of the world makes
himself an enemy of God.*

JAMES 4:4, NASB

When James talks about friendship with the world, what exactly does he
mean? He's talking about my longings for the things of this world and
any unhealthy attachments with someone or something, anything that
causes me to violate my relationship with God.

When it comes to my work, Lord, I realize that I must apply myself
according to Your spiritual and scriptural rules of engagement. My commitment to my workplace is not unlike a marriage. If I work in an office
where the people conduct business in a way that is biblically out of
order, then I must ask You how I can effect change—or I must seek
Your will in separating myself from the ungodly alliance.

The same applies to my friendships in the workplace. I must be
very careful with whom I choose to align myself. I want godly relationships, a work ethic of integrity, and holy alliances. For I shudder at the
thought of having *God* as my enemy!

"'Woe to the obstinate children,' declares the LORD, 'to those who
carry out plans that are not mine, forming an alliance, but not by my
Spirit, heaping sin upon sin; who go down to Egypt without consulting
me; who look for help to Pharaoh's protection, to Egypt's shade for
refuge. But Pharaoh's protection will be to your shame, Egypt's shade
will bring you disgrace'" (Isaiah 30:1-3, NIV).

Action Point: Today I tap into my friendship with God by leaning
on Him for comfort and direction.

CONFIDENTIALITY

As a ring of gold in a swine's snout, so is a lovely woman who lacks discretion.

PROVERBS 11:22

Gold is classically stylish and beautiful, yet no one would say of a pig with a fourteen-carat necklace, "Oh, look! How lovely!" Like Porky sliding a gold ring through his nose, so are people who lack discretion. They may appear valuable, but their true worth is evident in their lack of judgment. Some things just don't need to be repeated.

The temptation to disclose information, especially at work, can be irresistible. Everyone always wants to know or be in the know, preferably before anyone else. Getting caught up in the water-cooler conversation is part of the corporate culture, but as a Christian, I must be careful not to drown in it. I must be concerned not only about what I speak but also about what I permit myself to hear. Sometimes standing there listening to gossip is as damaging as the gossip itself. Do I want to be grouped with the gang known for indiscretion? Discretion is about keeping confidences, whether I'm in the know or out of it.

Lord, help me to be ever mindful of what to speak, when to speak, and the way and tone of my speech. Even if I feel as if I'm bursting at the seams because I know something that no one else does, may I be quick to listen and slow to speak, seeking at all times to bring about the righteous life that You are perfecting in me (see James 1:4,19).

Action Point: Today I excuse myself from any indiscreet conversation of which I know I should not be a part.

FALSE WITNESS

A false witness shall perish, but the man who hears him will speak endlessly.

PROVERBS 21:28

False witness is indiscretion taken to the extreme. When I speak of another person, especially in a community environment like the workplace, I had better speak the truth. God is holding me accountable for every single word that I speak (see Matthew 12:36-37).

Therefore, let me be mindful when I talk about a colleague, a coworker, or my supervisor. Let me be thoughtful before I speak about another's work. Let me ask the Holy Spirit to direct my mouth before bringing into question someone else's habits, style, or abilities. The tongue is capable of starting terrible fires (see James 3:6)!

Let me never bear false witness against another, because according to His Word, I will perish if I do, and the person I share the information with will speak about it endlessly. By speaking lies I perpetuate rumors; I spread bad yeast through a batch of unbaked bread. "Your boasting is not good. Don't you know that a little yeast works through the whole batch of dough?" (1 Corinthians 5:6, NIV).

It is so easy to get caught up in the conversation. So easy to want to add my little two cents. I have to decide daily to change my conversation. I can't afford to be out of order with the Lord just to be "in" with those who don't necessarily know the God I serve.

Lord, I want to serve You "in spirit and truth," and that means every day I must watch what I say (John 4:23).

Action Point: Today I ask the Holy Spirit to convict me of lies and put a clamp on my tongue before they ever leave my lips.

GOSSIP

A gossip betrays a confidence; so avoid a man who talks too much.

PROVERBS 20:19, NIV

I suspect that if a person is willing to tell me all about somebody else's business on the job, he's more than willing to offer up my business to someone else. No wonder Your Word tells me to avoid such a person! Remind me to never, ever trust a gossip. And, even more important, please strengthen my commitment to Your ways so that I never, ever become one.

Whatever I call it—gossip, office politics, water-cooler conversation—there is nothing "cool" about gossip. Instead, it is an effective tool, pervasive in the corporate culture, used to plant seeds of destruction.

God takes gossiping very seriously, and so should I, for His Word likens gossip to the heat of a roaring fire: "As charcoal to embers and as wood to fire, so is a quarrelsome man for kindling strife" (Proverbs 26:21, NIV).

Not only that, but "the words of a gossip are like choice morsels; they go down to a man's inmost parts" (verse 22, NIV). In those inmost parts, the abundance of my heart is formed. "For out of the abundance of the heart the mouth speaks" (Matthew 12:34).

Lord, let me speak only good from the abundance of a heart that is yielded to You.

Action Point: Today if I am tempted to gossip, I flee from the temptation and ask God to expose and heal the heart condition that gave temptation opportunity.

GRACE

Walk in wisdom toward those who are outside, redeeming the time. Let your speech always be with grace, seasoned with salt, that you may know how you ought to answer each one.

COLOSSIANS 4:5-6

How I desire the conversations I share with coworkers to be conversations full of grace, the grace of blessings I can offer with my words. The Bible says that "the tongue has the power of life and death" (Proverbs 18:21, NIV). Therefore, when I speak, I want to speak only words of life. If someone asks "How are you today?" may my reply be "Blessed." If someone makes a request, may my reaction be "I'm happy to see what I can do for you." If someone lodges a complaint, may I respond with "Let's talk about things so we can resolve the issue." My conversation need not be defensive or defenseless. I choose to change my conversation, knowing that when I do, He will change any confrontation. I can therefore speak reasonably, assuredly, and effectively.

May my conversations with my associates be seasoned with salt. The Word of God says that "salt is good" (Luke 14:34). The Word of God shows me that salt purifies (see 2 Kings 2:20-22). The Word of God tells me that I am "the salt of the earth" (Matthew 5:13). Let my conversations bring light where there is darkness at work. Lord, I want my words to produce good fruit that brings You glory. Pure conversations. Clear and concise communications. Where there is confusion, there is chaos; where there is grace, salt, and love, there is God.

Action Point: Today I make a conscious effort to bless a colleague with grace-filled conversation.

GRIEF

And do not grieve the Holy Spirit of God, by whom you were sealed for the day of redemption. Let all bitterness, wrath, anger, clamor, and evil speaking be put away from you, with all malice. And be kind to one another, tender-hearted, forgiving one another, even as God in Christ forgave you.

EPHESIANS 4:30-32

Sometimes grief overtakes me like a billowing wave rolling in from rough seas. At other times I am the wave, causing others to grieve because of what I say, do, or fail to do (see 2 Corinthians 2:5, NIV). Causing pain and mourning loss are a part of life, and while I am human with feelings and emotions, faults and frailties, I want to always be especially sensitive never to grieve the Holy Spirit.

When I am short-tempered, quick to criticize, or eager to make myself look good at the expense of others, I grieve the Holy Spirit. When I am prompted by the Spirit of God to share a word of admonition or encouragement but instead keep my mouth shut, I grieve the Holy Spirit. When I do things in excess that I know are not good for me, I grieve the Holy Spirit because the Spirit lives inside of me (see 1 Corinthians 3:16).

Lord, I want to please Your Holy Spirit. Protect my heart against bitterness. Help me to be slow to anger. Father, curb my tongue when I am tempted to talk about others. Give me patience, kindness, and a forgiving heart this day and every day so I don't grieve You by falling short of Your expectations for me.

Action Point: Today I act on the Spirit's promptings to bless another person in an unexpected way.

INFLUENCE

We know that we are of God, and the whole world lies under the sway of the wicked one.

1 JOHN 5:19

As a child of God, I am a sojourner in a foreign land (see 1 Peter 2:11). The Word tells us that the whole world is under the sway of the devil. That being the case, I must watch, look, and listen carefully to ensure that my sojourn is not influenced by evil. If I surround myself with godly influences at work and at home, I stand a better chance of making it through. I want to be truly influenced only by those who are "doers of the word, and not hearers only" (James 1:22).

As a follower of Christ, I also want to be a positive role model for someone who may not yet know God. I realize that my walk with Christ should be one in which others can see real growth in me, the result of my belief in the Word of God. I not only believe, but I achieve change when I seek to do His will in His way and in His timing.

I know that others may talk about me, even seek to undermine my work, but I still want to influence them positively. My actions should speak volumes about my personal character and about my God, especially to those who may not align themselves with my beliefs. Why? Because on the day when they meet God face to face, one on one, they will remember my good works and glorify my Father (see 1 Peter 2:12). So, Lord, help me now because You know I need it. Help me submit to You, commit to Your ways, and be a godly influence upon someone at work today.

Action Point: Today I examine the profound influences in my life and ask God how to replace the negative with the positive.

SPIRITUAL INTERVIEW

There was a man of the Pharisees named Nicodemus, a ruler of the Jews. This man came to Jesus by night and said to Him, "Rabbi, we know that You are a teacher come from God; for no one can do these signs that You do unless God is with him."

JOHN 3:1-2

Nicodemus was a very well-off man, well respected, well known, and a member of the Jewish ruling council. The council despised Jesus. Yet Nicodemus could not disregard such a man as Christ. Nicodemus was so moved while in Jesus' company that later he actively sought Him out for a one-on-one interview.

Why? Nicodemus was impressed by that man who spoke with such authority! Overwhelmed by the way Jesus handled Himself in high-pressure situations, Nicodemus was absolutely bowled over with awe because of the signs and wonders Jesus performed. So Nicodemus took a risk and went to be in Jesus' presence.

As I mature in my walk at work, I hope people will see the Lord's grace and power in my life and want to know more about Him. When individuals see those traits in me and want to know more about who I am, what I believe, and who I represent, I hope to interact with them as Jesus interacted with Nicodemus. John 3 describes a question-and-answer session that is natural, direct, and to the point. That is how I want to be: authentic! Not caught up in slick presentations, five-syllable words, or putting on airs. I will simply do what Jesus did.

Action Point: Today I read John 3 and ask God to give me a heart of compassion for people who on the inside are seeking Christ but on the outside may not be able to express it.

LANGUAGE

But now you yourselves are to put off all these: anger, wrath, malice, blasphemy, filthy language out of your mouth. Do not lie to one another, since you have put off the old man with his deeds, and have put on the new man who is renewed in knowledge according to the image of Him who created him.

COLOSSIANS 3:8-10

Putting off "the old man with his deeds" is like trying to shake a piece of gum off my shoe. Every time I take a step, that sticky mess stays with me. That's what living in the flesh means. All my filthy attitudes and actions are stuck to my soul, and sometimes I'm so covered in them that I can't even see how to clean myself up. Yet, as a child of God and an imitator of Christ, I long to become more like Him each day.

Cleaning up my spirit of its fleshy messes requires action. One of the things that require vigilant cleaning is my language. The words I speak should reflect Christ's lordship over my life. If I want to make progress in my walk, I can ask the Lord to help me tailor my language to be more Christlike. "Out of the same mouth proceed blessing and cursing. My brethren, these things ought not to be so" (James 3:10). The apostle James also tells us that no man can tame the tongue because it is full of deadly poison. Filthy words can only be filtered out through the power of the Holy Spirit.

Action Point: Today I ask for the power to learn the language of love lest I hurt someone's spirit with my words.

COMMIT Through Prayer and Praise

Be anxious for nothing, but in everything by prayer and supplication, with thanksgiving, let your requests be made known to God; and the peace of God, which surpasses all understanding, will guard your hearts and minds through Christ Jesus.

Philippians 4:6-7

As we make every effort to fulfill our commitments to our colleagues and employers, prayer plays a critical role. I know because I'm an eleventh-hour person. I have a plate full of responsibilities, ventures, and ideas, as well as the heartfelt desire to be available to God whenever He calls. So it's inevitable that I leave a few things until the very last minute! As I pen these very words, I am scheduled to have the manuscript to the most patient of editors. Yep. Today is Deadline Day. For the past five weeks, I have been operating solely by the power of the Holy Spirit and sheer determination. God is pressing me to live out this fourth step of S.U.C.C.E.S.S.: *Commitment.* You see, I agreed that I would have the book to the publisher by a particular date. I not only confessed out of my mouth, but I also contractually signed. So, in my mind, there was never a question about whether I would have it done. I knew I would do what it took, no matter the cost. After coming to the end of me, a place we all need to be, I just had to pray: "Thy will be done."

Of course, *praying* for God's will should be natural in a Christian's life. If we don't want what He has to offer, then what's the point of calling Him Lord? However, *accepting* His will is where we move from simply talking about our faith to walking out our faith. It is in this place that we all are challenged to obey. "But this is what I commanded them, saying, 'Obey My voice, and I will be your God, and you shall be My people. And walk in all the ways that I have commanded you, that it may be well with you'" (Jeremiah 7:23).

The Midnight Hour

And at midnight Paul and Silas prayed, and sang praises unto God: and the prisoners heard them. And suddenly there was a great earthquake, so that the foundations of the prison were shaken: and immediately all the doors were opened, and everyone's bands were loosed. (Acts 16:25-26, KJV)

Just as God has proven faithful to me in the eleventh hour, I have found that God is also faithful in the midnight hour, in those dark seasons of our lives when we don't know what to do next. When the time came for me to write this chapter, I didn't really have a clue where to begin. I just sat here—tired, weary, and exhausted. After about ten minutes, I realized I must start by turning to the Source. Kneeling down with my head resting on my office chair, I whispered, "Oh, Lord, I thank You, heavenly Father, that I can come to You in my hour of need. You know I can't make it through without You. I am at the end of me, but You have no end, for You are the Alpha and the Omega. Thank You, Lord. I am so privileged to be used by Your Holy Spirit to write a book about You! A book that I pray will lead others to Your Son, Jesus Christ. A guide that I want to be authentic, effective, and read daily in order to equip the people of God to deal with everyday life at work. I'm asking for an extra portion of Your grace. I'm asking for an extra portion of Your wisdom. I'm asking for an extra portion of discernment. And, Lord, please energize me to get through and let me be open to no other voice but Yours. In the name of Jesus, I pray. Amen."

Well, do I have to tell you? God is so faithful! My heavy eyes opened up. My lifeless fingers began to dance across the keyboard. My mind became unclouded without my mocha java! And thanks to the spiritual caffeine, the Holy Spirit, coursing through my veins, I became energized.

I can't begin to tell you how many times the Lord has, as my friend Jestacia is fond of saying, "shown up and showed out." By that she means He comes through in a big way—in a way that we could never imagine for ourselves. When we ask God to intervene, He will, and when He does, we can know that He has handled our circumstances in our best interest.

At times God answers our petitions right away, but at other times we cannot see His provision. Then we must simply trust that He will take care of us. Our prayer lives remain healthy when we remember that God is the Timekeeper in our lives. His answers to our prayers will always come when we need them most. Whether His answers are speedy or seemingly delayed, we can find encouragement in the truth that He has brought us through every situation in life before and that He will continue to do so now. We can patiently wait on Him, understanding that the interim between prayer and answered prayer should cause us to lean more and more on our Perfect God and to rest in Him. We should never allow our frustrations in prayer to cause us to fall or fail. If we lose heart and do things our way rather than wait patiently or respond obediently, we won't progress very far: "Yet they did not obey or incline their ear, but followed the counsels and the dictates of their evil hearts, and went backward and not forward" (Jeremiah 7:24).

When I look back on my times of need, I see that it wasn't up to me to orchestrate how the Lord would answer a prayer. It was up to me simply to say "Yes, Lord" when He asked something of me. So the next time you find yourself at the midnight hour, remember that this is the time to trust the most, pray the hardest, say "Yes, Lord," and praise Him for answering your prayers.

Praying for, Not About

> Let love be without hypocrisy. Abhor what is evil. Cling to what
> is good. Be kindly affectionate to one another with brotherly love,
> in honor giving preference to one another; not lagging in diligence,
> fervent in spirit, serving the Lord; rejoicing in hope, patient in
> tribulation, continuing steadfastly in prayer; distributing to the
> needs of the saints, given to hospitality. (Romans 12:9-13)

A friend of mine couldn't figure out why his boss had it in for him. It seemed that she just plain didn't like him. I couldn't imagine it either. I mean, Ed is a guy whom everybody likes. Yeah, he's a bit of a cutup. He can be funny and boyish, loud and bigger than life at times, but he's handsome, smart, articulate, and always ready to help anybody out. The guy's a genuine sweetheart, a Christian with a true desire to live for the Lord, but hey, he's walking day by day just as we all are.

His relationship with his boss eventually became so bad that he just couldn't bear the thought of going to work. By the end of each day, he was racing to get out of there. Ed loves his job, enjoys his work, is challenged by identifying problems and fixing them, but the boss presented him with one problem he hadn't been able to fix—her.

I told him, "Ed, you have to pray for her. I mean really pray *for* her, not *about* her." Have you ever gone to God *on* someone? You know— called on Him as you might call on your big brother to beat somebody up for messing with you? Sometimes our prayers sound a little like this: "God, You know I just can't take this person anymore. I don't know what's wrong with him, but if something doesn't happen soon, I'm gonna blow up. I'm going to march in and tell him off. He's rude and arrogant, and I'm not taking it anymore." Imagine how that sounds to God:

God, You know I just can't take this person anymore.

If I am patient with you, can't you be a little more patient with him?

I don't know what's wrong with him.

What's wrong with him is everything that was wrong with you before you met Me.

If something doesn't happen soon, I'm gonna blow up.

Well, with an ultimatum like that, I think I'll have to keep you there a little longer for you to develop a bit more patience.

I'm going to march in and tell him off.

And while I'm at it, how about a few more lessons to teach you to control that temper?

He's rude.

You're rebellious.

He's arrogant.

I'm sensing attitude here!

And I'm not dealing with it anymore.

Okay, let's take it from the top again… Who's in charge here?

Ed began to pray for his boss. Very shortly afterward, she was forced to take time off from work for a couple of weeks. Everything in her personal life seemed to be falling apart. Ed prayed for her health when she was physically challenged. He prayed for her family when her child went astray. He prayed for her to have peace in the midst of her personal storms. He even sent her an e-mail letting her know he was lifting her up in prayer. When she came back to work, Ed said to me, "Andria, it's as if she's a different person. I mean, she and I are talking, we're connecting, and her attitude is totally turned around. I just can't believe it! It's nothing but God!"

You see, the Lord calls His children to stand in the gap and pray for His other children. With each challenge, God is trying to grow us up. He is allowing every difficulty and can use each to be a building block to true S.U.C.C.E.S.S. Remember: We are to Seek, Unite, Change, Commit, Enjoy, Surrender, and Serve. You must take each step to success; none can be skipped. We have to apply each principle to our daily lives in order to fully serve God "in spirit and truth" (John 4:23-24).

Prayer is a major component leading to daily triumph at the office. It doesn't mean that every day will be Sunday, as they say, but it does mean that we will begin to recognize and then rejoice: Through faith and prayer, success will come day by day.

WHERE PRAYER MEETS SPIRITUAL COMMITMENT

But let your "Yes" be "Yes," and your "No," "No." (Matthew 5:37)

Devoting ourselves to prayer will help us find our success, namely, a certain detachment from the outcome of life's events. By *detachment* I mean acknowledging that we really don't want anything that God doesn't want for us. When we do that we can remain unaffected by life's challenges and the circumstances that don't seem to be going our way. We make our greatest spiritual commitment to God's desires for our life, no matter what His plan looks like.

In this season of my life, my aim is to remain open and committed to moving in the direction that God has chosen for me. Rather than getting stuck in the mind-set that true success will come about as the result of what *I* want for my life, I've released my will in order to accept His. With God as my CEO, I'm working daily to give up manipulating, orchestrating, and maneuvering circumstances and people in order to get what I want. The only thing I really want now is to be pliable enough for God to fashion me into the creation He desires.

Case in point: One of the greatest decisions of my life came after a revelation I had just before I left CNN. God had given me a celestial heads-up, if you will. I knew my time at CNN was drawing to a close. All signs were pointing me back to New Jersey, but if I left CNN, what would I do? How would I support myself and contribute to my family? Where would the money come from? This is where the testing of my faith came in. I had been confessing, "God is my Source. He's my Provision"—but was I going to believe it? Were my statements of faith merely lip service?

Now, I'm only telling you this next part because I know I can trust you. I also want you to know that each of us has some level of attachment to the world's value system. The question is: How much do we buy into it? My attachment has been tested time and time again, and the testing will continue as I serve Him. The same will be the case for you. The reason is nothing heavy or mysterious. Simply put, God wants us to be available to serve Him. If we're committed to *things,* but not to *Him,* our calendars fill up very quickly with attachments that distract us from that "one thing" that is better (Luke 10:42, KJV).

Not that I boast on my behalf, only in the Lord (see 2 Corinthians 11:30), but I was pulling down some pretty hefty cash. As a veteran broadcast journalist seen all around the world, I had a salary well into the six figures. Unless I went to work at another network, how was I ever going to match that? It's not as if my husband and I don't have bills, debt, a mortgage, responsibilities, and three kids—two of whom are already in braces, and the little one needs them real soon. The only answer was to press even more into prayer. I'd already traveled the "left my job, ain't got no money" route when I exited the NBC station in

New York to write my first book, and I really wasn't interested in taking that path again.

I was about to learn, however, that God *will* bring each of us right back around the same track as many times as necessary until we make the right choice about what we're going to believe: either our circumstances or the Word of God. And there's only one right answer.

A Dedication to the One I Love

> Commit to the LORD whatever you do, and your plans will
> succeed. (Proverbs 16:3, NIV)

Before I left CNN, I felt as if my personal life was totally upside down, so I began to pray for *God's* order and balance. What was *His* goal for me, and exactly how did He want me to achieve it?

The Lord directed me to resurrect the company I had established years before: SpeakEasy Communications—Media Coaching, Public Speaking, Video Production. This road would enable me to work primarily from home and be available to my family as a wife and mother. In terms of my business, I decided to stand on Proverbs 16:3, and I dedicated it to the Lord. God had blessed me with all good things (see James 1:17), and since I wanted everything to be in divine order, I knew I must give my company back to Him too.

Now, it's not like SpeakEasy was thriving when I had left it long ago for the job in Atlanta. On the contrary, its miniscule revenues accounted for why I needed a job in the first place. This time, however, would be different. I'd given up being politically correct; I just wanted to be biblically correct. The Lord prompted me to put things in order and incorporate. After all, for four years I had been conducting business under an unregistered name. I wasn't a "real" company.

Four months later, I learned that someone else in New Jersey owned the company name I had been using: SpeakEasy Communications. It was unavailable to me. I couldn't believe it! For a millisecond I was so disappointed, but I was not defeated. Clearly the Lord had something else in mind.

We can keep our balance even as God reveals a plan different from ours when we remain committed to our commitments. I needed to remain committed to the Lord and to what He had given me—the vision of a company that glorified Him. Commitment, I have learned, is the same in life, in love, and in our work: It is not a feeling; it is a decision.

So, with that door shut, I said, "Lord, it's obvious You must want to call this company something else. What would You like to name it?" That night I went to bed with that prayer. The Lord woke me up early the next morning. I headed to the computer and typed out this:

June 14, 2001

Praise Your holy and mighty name! Praise the name of Jesus! Thank you for the rebirth of SpeakEasy Communications. The Holy Spirit has ordained its new name, and it is rededicated to Him who is able to keep me from falling.

Father God, Jesus Christ, Holy Spirit, I present to You:

SpeakEasy M.E.D.I.A., Inc.
Ministering
Edifying
Divinely
Inspiring
All to the glory of God

Standing on the Word of God, from Ephesians 4:29: "Let no corrupt communication proceed out of your mouth, but that which is good to the use of edifying, that it may minister grace unto the hearers" (KJV).

I began to walk in God's divine direction because I desperately wanted to get to a place where my walk at work was working for all aspects of my life. (And, by the way, your walk at work should also be working for the people who employ you.) My prayer was for His guidance and strength. My desire to stay on course was consistent and fervent (see James 5:16). In response to my prayers and spiritual commitment, God made my path plain. Today SpeakEasy M.E.D.I.A. is a corporate entity working for His glory.

God will make your path plain for you just as He did for me. If you continue to seek the Lord's way of expediting His vision for your life, the Holy Spirit will guide you into the truth of what that is. Making a wholehearted commitment to the Lord is often the catalyst we need to begin clearing the clutter from our spiritual closets. Then we are able to see what He has in there for us.

Practical Application

However, when He, the Spirit of truth, has come, He will guide you into all truth; for He will not speak on His own authority, but whatever He hears He will speak; and He will tell you things to come. (John 16:13)

Want to move away from wishy-washy or aimless work to a marvelous mission designed to glorify Jesus Christ? Here is the path that worked for me:

- Listen! Jesus Christ is calling you to participate in His plan for your life.
- Commit your path to Him by learning to detach yourself from the world's perspective on success.
- Ask the Holy Spirit to clean up your spiritual closet—the cobwebs and clutter, the sin and confusion—by showing you what is in disarray.
- Seek God's order and balance for your life.
- Realize that you don't have to be perfect to serve Him because you serve a perfect God.
- Agree with God that His best for you is all you want.
- Get direction from the Holy Bible daily. Be sensitive to the voice of the Holy Spirit. Seek Christ-centered counsel.
- Commit your work to the Lord, so that everything you do is consciously intended to glorify Him.

Spiritual Truth

Continue earnestly in prayer, being vigilant in it with thanksgiving. (Colossians 4:2)

As Christians we are called to a life of prayer. Prayer in the workplace may not be politically correct, but it is spiritually correct, and it is a command by God to be obeyed.

Fourth Steps

- Pray with pure motivations from a pure heart: "You ask and do not receive, because you ask amiss, that you may spend it on your pleasures" (James 4:3).

- Choose to commit your work to Him. Commitment is not a feeling; it's a choice.
- Begin to conduct yourself according to Proverbs 16:3, NIV: "Commit to the Lord whatever you do, and your plans will succeed."

Journal Exercises

- Write down the most serious prayer needs you see in your place of work. Then, as time goes by, write down—based on His Word—what you desire the Lord to change in your work environment.
- Next, ask God's *best* for the person you like *least* at work. Do it with all your heart, realizing that God wants all "to be saved and to come to the knowledge of the truth" (1 Timothy 2:3-4).

I Exalt Thee!

Praise Your name, O God. I lift my heart song to You.

My inner spirit resounds with an awesome love for You.

So sweet are the silent whispers of Your Spirit in my ear.

You have given me a prayer to sing

While on bended knee—I know You're there.

I exalt Thee... I exalt Thee, O God... I exalt Thee
    evermore.

My heart is Yours, O God.

Please hear my song of praise.

Receive my prayer with gladness;

Incline Your ear to hear me this day.

This is a servant's weak attempt

To worship and adore Thee, You, a perfect God,

Who now and forever will be.

For You, O God, defy description.

You alone are worthy to be praised.

Let me sing aloud to those around me.

Let me cause them to see Your face.

Nothing any man could ever do would cause me

to turn away from You.

In prayer, no matter what the time,

I thank You, for I am Yours and You are mine,

I exalt Thee... I exalt Thee...

Sweet Jesus, I exalt Thee.

Amen.

ADVERSITY

And a great windstorm arose, and the waves beat into the boat, so that it was already filling. But He was in the stern, asleep on a pillow. And they awoke Him and said to Him, "Teacher, do You not care that we are perishing?" Then He arose and rebuked the wind, and said to the sea, "Peace, be still!"

MARK 4:37-39

Even though I live and work in Christ, my faith will not shield me completely from adversity. Great storms are going to arise as I walk with the Lord. The wind may blow and beat me down, even stir up the waters of change around me. I may be overwhelmed to the point I fear drowning, but I have faith that God is with me (see Joshua 1:9).

Our Lord has said, "I will never leave you nor forsake you" (Hebrews 13:5), and in the midst of the storm, I stand firm on that promise. Circumstances may attempt to dilute my commitment. Coworkers may ostracize me. Supervisors may criticize me and try to stop me, but none of that matters if I simply stay in the boat with Jesus. All that is important is that I remember He is with me, capable of rebuking any storm. He will wait for my faith in Him to kick in, and He will respond.

Let me not complicate what might appear to be a difficult circumstance. The simple fact is that God is in charge, and His Truth prevails. His peace allows me to be still despite some pretty rough waters.

Action Point: Today, in the face of trials, I envision myself in the safety of a boat captained by Jesus.

Burnout

And He rested on the seventh day from all His work which He had done. Then God blessed the seventh day and sanctified it, because in it He rested from all His work.

Genesis 2:2-3

I really ought to know better by now. I really ought to be able to see the warning signs announcing "Burnout!" ahead *before* I reach the crossroads where my only choices are sickness or emotional breakdown. After all, my need to unplug completely and rest totally is right there in the Word: "And He rested on the seventh day from all His work." Not part of His work, but *all!*

Lord, help me to understand and embrace Your principle for regular and complete rest. Father, help me mature to the point where I don't feel guilty if I'm not busy doing, moving, or giving.

Yes, work is demanding at times, and certainly life generates its own perpetual motion that expects my constant attention. But I must get to a place where I practice regular weekly intervals of pure rest. Thank You, Lord, for giving me permission to be still and know that You are God (see Psalm 46:10). I will rest with You when I unplug from the world and abstain from *all* my work.

Action Point: Today I plan a day of complete rest for myself sometime within the next two weeks.

ABSTINENCE

Abstain from every form of evil.

1 THESSALONIANS 5:22

The Word of God gives me instruction for good living, righteous living, and holy living. First Thessalonians 5:16-22 tells me I should:

- rejoice always.
- pray without ceasing.
- give thanks in everything.
- never quench the Spirit.
- not despise prophecies.
- test all things.
- hold fast to what is good.
- *abstain from every form of evil.*

The Bible also uses the term *abstinence* when instructing me about things I should avoid. If I stay close to God by studying His Word, my discernment in this area will grow. It's easy to get caught up in office politics, corporate culture, idle chat, gossip, sexual temptation, and backbiting, but as a believer, I want to avoid such things, knowing they will separate me from God. If I can't build up a colleague, I must refuse to tear him or her down. Instead, I will seek unity with my coworkers by rejoicing in all things, praying without ceasing, always giving thanks to God (even for trials), being sensitive to the Holy Spirit, listening to godly counsel, testing all things according to the Word of God, and holding fast to what is good. If it's not edifying, I will abstain from it— no matter what "it" is.

Action Point: Today I ask God for wisdom to discern what is evil and for the strength to stay away from it.

ENDURANCE

Blessed is the man who endures temptation; for when he has been proved, he will receive the crown of life which the Lord has promised to those who love Him.

JAMES 1:12

Work is definitely one place where temptations abound. My inner strength is often challenged, and moment by moment my ethics could be put on trial. Rather than fall prey to temptation, I fix my eyes on the promise God has for me if I endure. So today I confess that:

- I will not give in to the temptation to cut corners in any area of my work, even when I know I can get away with doing less, because I realize that effort would not be my best.
- I will not give in to the temptation to elevate myself above a colleague, because the Lord asks me to treat others as better than myself.
- I will not give in to sexual temptation. I am aware how easy it can be to develop inappropriate relationships on the job.

God knows all things. He peers deep into my heart, weighing my intent and motivations to see if they support my commitment to Him. Lord, equip me to press through until the end. Father, I desire Your stamp of approval on my life. I want a crown of glory, Your blessing. Evidence of my love for You is simply to do what You say to do. So I continue until my testing is over, and I patiently wait on Your promise. Lord Jesus, help me to endure this day at work. Help me to do so with joy so I can receive Your blessed approval.

Action Point: Today I pray for strength to endure professional pressure in whatever form it presents itself to me.

THE ART OF LISTENING

Now so it was that after three days they found Him in the temple, sitting in the midst of the teachers, both listening to them and asking them questions. And all who heard Him were astonished at His understanding and answers.

LUKE 2:46-47

When Jesus was only twelve years old, He had mastered a very important skill: the art of listening. While sitting in the presence of scholarly men, theologians, and Old Testament philosophers, He realized at just twelve years old that God had given Him two ears and one mouth—as we say—so that He could listen twice as much as He spoke.

Jesus listened first, and then He asked questions. The natural outpouring of that attentiveness was a positive reaction from those around Him. They were amazed both that He understood them and that His insights were so profound. At work I sometimes find myself in the presence of some pretty heavy hitters. Just like Jesus (although admittedly I am not very much like Jesus!), I need not feel intimidated or apprehensive.

Maybe I have a meeting with my supervisor today, maybe the president, perhaps even a partner. In all my conversations, I will seek to understand the issues first. So, Lord, before I open my mouth to speak, please prepare me to speak appropriately. Above all, teach me how to listen to You so that I can grasp the truth. When I listen well to others and to You, I will have so much more to offer, and when I do speak, others will want to hear what I have to say.

Action Point: No matter whom I encounter today, I make every effort to listen more than I talk.

EFFORT

How can you believe if you accept praise from one another, yet make no effort to obtain the praise that comes from the only God?

JOHN 5:44, NIV

Saying "I believe in God" is one of the easiest confessions I can make. Earnestly seeking God's will and praise, however, is an altogether different matter. That kind of commitment requires faith, consistency, tolerance, patience, and daily effort.

In the workplace, it seems that everyone is always seeking to be acknowledged for his or her efforts. If a project goes well, someone is always willing to stand and take credit. If a deadline is met, of course it was because of dedicated effort. Daily we want others to recognize what we bring to the table and compensate us accordingly, whether in praise or with a raise.

Lord, accepting the praises of another is a natural desire, but I want to have supernatural yearnings. I would rather seek Your praises, O God, than that of mere men who will remember my efforts only for a time; You, Lord, remember for always. I want to make a daily effort to please You, first by living with a faith-filled heart (see Hebrews 11:6) and, second, by working always for You (see Colossians 3:23, NIV). Let everything I do in word or deed be done in the name of the Lord Jesus Christ, for His glory alone, as I give thanks to You, Lord God, through Your precious Son. Let me make every effort to merit Your praises, remembering that the only reward that counts is that You approve of me and are well pleased with my service.

Action Point: Today I seek the praises of God rather than the praises of men by performing to His standard and to the best of my ability.

MATURITY

Not that I have already attained, or am already perfected; but I press on, that I may lay hold of that for which Christ Jesus has also laid hold of me. Brethren, I do not count myself to have apprehended; but one thing I do, forgetting those things which are behind and reaching forward to those things which are ahead, I press toward the goal for the prize of the upward call of God in Christ Jesus. Therefore let us, as many as are mature, have this mind.

PHILIPPIANS 3:12-15

Father, help me not to become conceited in my Christianity. Lord Jesus, keep me from presenting myself as if I've always had my spiritual act together because, Lord, You and I both know the whole story. If it weren't for Your continued grace, where would I be? Little more than a baby struggling to digest the pure milk of the Word (see Hebrews 5:12-14).

I know You want me to mature in my relationship with You, so I press on. I know You want me to bring You into the center of my everyday work experience, so I press on. I believe You smile down at me from heaven each time I react to work challenges as a mature follower of Christ, seeking Your will even in the midst of my trials. So for every step I take, I am reminded to "lay hold of that for which Christ Jesus has also laid hold of me." Your Holy Spirit whispers to my soul, "Press on." The more of my old self I leave behind, the deeper I move into knowing You. The more I reach forward to those things which are ahead, the more I realize that while I will never attain full maturity this side of heaven, by Your grace I am growing day by day. I strive to make you proud.

Action Point: Today I view my trials as a tool God can use to bring about my perfect maturity in Him.

LIGHT

You are the light of the world. A city that is set on a hill cannot be hidden. Nor do they light a lamp and put it under a basket, but on a lampstand, and it gives light to all who are in the house. Let your light so shine before men, that they may see your good works and glorify your Father in heaven.

MATTHEW 5:14-16

As a believer, I am called the "light of the world." As a follower of Christ in the workplace, I am moved to shine brightly so that others will see my good works. There's only one reason for me to shine: It's not for pride. It's not for boasting. It's not for self-aggrandizement or ego boosting.

I am to perform "good works" for the sole purpose of "glorifying my Father in heaven." Pride would have me take the credit every time I do something worthwhile, but the Word makes it abundantly clear: If I am even tempted to take a bow for a job well done, I must listen to the warning of the apostle James: "Do not be deceived, my beloved brethren. Every good gift and every perfect gift is from above, and comes down from the Father of lights, with whom there is no variation or shadow of turning" (1:16-17).

God's wonderful and glorious way is that He never changes, not even a tiny bit. God is apolitical. Only the light of "right" emanates from Him. May the light of my works and my witness shine brightly before my coworkers so that they may discover the way to Him who is the Creator of every good thing in me. Let me show them Jesus!

Action Point: Today I prayerfully commit my works to the shining purposes of God so that they will have the effect He desires in the lives of others.

QUESTIONS

Now when the queen of Sheba heard of the fame of Solomon concerning the name of the LORD, she came to test him with hard questions.

1 KINGS 10:1

Whenever people test me by questioning my faith in the Lord, I pray that I will be able to follow this guidance from the Word: "Be ready in season and out of season. Convince, rebuke, exhort, with all longsuffering and teaching" (2 Timothy 4:2).

The queen of Sheba went to Solomon specifically to ask him the hard questions. She wanted to know about the Lord of Israel. She wanted to find out just how blessed Solomon really was and whether all she had heard about him was true. I should expect that when people see my spiritual wealth they will want to know about my beliefs and my blessings, too. When someone comes to me with the "hard questions," may my commitment to Your Word effectively equip me to:

- Convince: Let my convictions come through strong and clear.
- Rebuke: No matter what they throw at me, help me to answer them satisfactorily with the truth of God's Word.
- Exhort: May I be able to encourage them with the truth of Jesus Christ and what it means to be His disciple.

I will lift up the name of the Most Holy God in hopes that they will lift up praise to You, just as the queen of Sheba did when Solomon satisfied her curiosity about His God: "Blessed be the LORD your God, who delighted in you" (1 Kings 10:9).

Action Point: Today I read the Word carefully, so I can answer questions with accurate and passionate conviction.

CONSCIENCE

Pray for us; for we are confident that we have a good conscience, in all things desiring to live honorably.

HEBREWS 13:18

Ahhh, the joy of a clear conscience. It comes about only by one thing, and that is living a life aligned with God's Word. As I review the Ten Commandments (see Exodus 20), I realize that not one of us has lived up to them all. But for me yesterday is gone, and tomorrow has not yet come. So today I desire to do what it takes to have a clear and clean conscience. God wants to use the bright beam of His light to expose what is dark in me (see John 12:46).

Lord, please give me the courage to bring my full self into Your Light. I stand before You today in the righteousness of Christ, which means I have been made clean by the blood of Jesus. Being in right standing with You means I can have a clean conscience by all the power and authority given me by Jesus Christ (see Luke 10:19).

- My conscience is clear when I renounce and repent of those wrong things I have done, and ask the Lord for forgiveness and to do better by the power of the Holy Spirit.
- My conscience is clear when I seek God's will and then do it!
- My conscience is clear when I speak Christlike words in love.
- My conscience is clear when I do all I can to point others to Jesus Christ.
- My conscience is clear when the choices I make please God.

Action Point: Today I ask God to use His light to search my heart and expose any darkness there so that I can walk in His way without the baggage of hidden sin (see Psalm 139:23-24).

FAMILY

But if anyone does not provide for his own, and especially for those of his household, he has denied the faith and is worse than an unbeliever.

1 TIMOTHY 5:8

I work, Father, because I want Your will for my life. Each morning I get up and start my workday because I seek provision for myself and for my family. I want to do well, Lord, because You call me to excellence and have given me great hopes and dreams.

But there are times when I'm just plain tired, and it seems that I never have enough time to be with the family You've blessed me with. How can I scale back and still attend to all the responsibilities You've set before me? It sometimes seems impossible to give all I need to.

Your Word calls for me to provide for my household. You expect me to provide financially, physically, and, most important, spiritually. So while my job threatens to devour more and more of my time, talents, and abilities, I will remember that "I can do all things through Christ who strengthens me" (Philippians 4:13). I choose at this very moment to redefine success as looking only to You for validation and seeking only Your will for myself and my family.

Help me, Holy Spirit, to balance all the demands I have at work with the needs my family has at home. Thank You, Jesus, for showing me that provision entails more than making money. Provision also includes enabling my family to experience deeper faith in You and greater love for one another.

Action Point: Today I guard my family's needs by saying no to a request that would interfere with my commitment to them.

CALLING

Did you not know that I must be about My Father's business?

LUKE 2:49

Is that You, Jesus, calling me? Is that You, Jesus, whispering in my ear? In order for me to hear the voice of Jesus, I must tune my heart to the frequency of His Spirit. I must tune everything else out and open my heart to hearing from Him. I must put in the time and wait on the Lord, put all else on hold, and listen for His call.

The world calls to me too, and its call presents a great challenge. My job, my family, my friends, and my life all call me to move toward them and away from Him. But when Jesus calls, I want to obey. Just as He was, "I must be about My Father's business." His business takes me into the garden, where I tend my relationship with Him. Lord, help me daily to pluck up the weeds that grow there. I want to uproot those things that try to choke my commitment to Your calling.

Help me also to keep Your priorities straight. My calling is not necessarily my work. And my calling is not necessarily to support everyone else all the time. My calling is to do whatever it takes to stay close to You, underneath Your wings, listening to Your heartbeat, and resting in the comfort of Your everlasting arms. When I listen daily for my calling, I listen for instructions on what to do, when to do it, and how to do it.

Lord, sharpen my ability to hear You to the point where the world's voice no longer distracts me. Bring clarity to my calling as well as my work. When You are my top priority, all my other responsibilities will fall into order, and my work will be fruitful.

Action Point: Today I feast on God's Word as the first step toward learning to hear Him clearly.

GOOD INTENTIONS

The kingdom of heaven is like a man who sowed good seed in his field; but while men slept, his enemy came and sowed tares among the wheat and went his way. But when the grain had sprouted and produced a crop, then the tares also appeared.

MATTHEW 13:24-26

My good intention is to go into the field of the world and sow good seed wherever I walk. Although this good intention may motivate me, I need always be aware of the cold and callous heart of the evil one, who always wants to sabotage my good intentions.

The devil will try to creep into my world and sow seeds of anger, doubt, disobedience, and disaster, and before I know it, among my good intentions will spring up weeds of dissension. I see this happen all too easily at work! I start on a project, and someone else tries to derail it. I try to exercise self-control under the weights of deadlines and other pressures, and unforeseen circumstances try my patience and my faith.

Faced with these circumstances, I will listen to the parable of Jesus and ask God for the wisdom to understand the mysteries He speaks. While my good intentions must coexist with the "tares" of life, there will come a time when the Spirit of God will bring forth the harvest, and when He does, my faithfulness to Him will speak for me. If I stay the course, tend to my field, constantly monitor my good intentions, and guard against the enemy, then the wheat of my crop will be useful in the kingdom of God.

Action Point: Today I am on guard against the devil's attempts to sow weeds in my life.

PROBLEM SOLVER

*"Now I have heard that you are able to give interpretations and to
solve difficult problems. If you can read this writing and tell me
what it means, you will be clothed in purple and have a gold chain
placed around your neck, and you will be made the third highest
ruler in the kingdom."*

*Then Daniel answered the king, "You may keep your gifts for
yourself and give your rewards to someone else. Nevertheless, I will
read the writing for the king and tell him what it means."*

DANIEL 5:16-17, NIV

Lord, let me be known as a problem solver. When I show up for work
each day, let my reputation for excellence and my desire to provide
answers precede me. I make these requests not because I want to be show-
ered with favor or riches, but because I look to You for a greater reward.

Daniel was a prophet known to solve difficult problems. Like
Daniel, I want to be known for discerning the issues, completing tasks,
and offering up spiritual wisdom even in the most adverse circumstances. I thank You, Lord, that no problem is too big for You to solve,
no issue too complex for You to resolve, no challenge too great for You
to meet, no day too dark for Your light to shine through.

Like Daniel, I want to be known as a problem solver. After all, the
truth of the matter is, when I lean on You and not on my own understanding, when I acknowledge You in all my ways, You are faithful and
sure to direct my path (see Proverbs 3:5-6).

Action Point: Today I approach my problems as a gift from God, an
opportunity to gain wisdom for His glory.

QUITTING

Refrain your voice from weeping, and your eyes from tears; for your work shall be rewarded, says the LORD, and they shall come back from the land of the enemy. There is hope in your future.

JEREMIAH 31:16-17

On days when I feel like quitting, I will reflect on these words of the Lord. I will quiet my tears and dry my eyes. His words are my strength, and I delight in the promises of God. *My work shall be rewarded.* For this reason I will keep my commitments. Even if not one single individual appreciates what I do or recognizes my strengths, talents, or abilities, God does. Being in right standing with Him is really all that matters, for He will strengthen me whenever I am dismayed. He will uphold me with His "righteous right hand" (Isaiah 41:10).

I have felt like getting off the treadmill plenty of times. I have longed to find more meaningful employment, more fulfilling work. But in these times, if I remind myself of my Father's words, I can rejoice. "'For I know the plans I have for you,' declares the LORD, 'plans to prosper you and not to harm you, plans to give you hope and a future. Then you will call upon me and come and pray to me, and I will listen to you'" (Jeremiah 29:11-12, NIV).

Action Point: Today I refuse to quit. Instead, I go to God and pray to Him, then embrace His strengthening words for me.

HEART DESIRE

Now the Pharisees, who were lovers of money, were listening to all these things and were scoffing at Him. And He said to them, "You are those who justify yourselves in the sight of men, but God knows your hearts; for that which is highly esteemed among men is detestable in the sight of God."

LUKE 16:14-15, NASB

Jesus gives warning to all those who are puffed up with pride, who are lovers of money, and who make fun of Him and His teachings. God, who sees it all, knows what's inside the hearts of men. The second part of His admonition is a thought for me to hang on to: "That which is highly esteemed among men is detestable in the sight of God."

What is in my heart? Is it detestable to God? What do I esteem? As I look around me, I see so many things that others proclaim good. There is a better car in the parking lot than mine. Someone has a corner office with a view. Don't even get me started on the paycheck!

Lord, whenever I begin to entertain thoughts that line up with what everybody else holds dear and then justify those thoughts with reasons and excuses, let me draw back and draw near to You. For I know that status, position, wealth, and power—anything "that exalts itself against the knowledge" of You (2 Corinthians 10:5)—I am to cast down. If it is deeply valued by the world, it is not just disgusting to You, but despicable! Moreover, when in my heart I try to justify how I might get these very same things by means that don't line up with Your ways, convict me. I want my heart to please you.

Action Point: Today I pay attention to the desires of my heart and ask God to help me by giving me the desires of His heart.

DETERMINATION

For I determined not to know anything among you except Jesus Christ and Him crucified.

1 CORINTHIANS 2:2

Sometimes I can be so determined just to make it. So determined to argue my point or to have my way that I fail in the most basic biblical principles.

It is my desire that my most fundamental determination, on the job and elsewhere, is to focus on the Lord Jesus Christ and Him crucified. It is He who died for me. It is He whom I seek to please. So daily I ask, Lord, what do You want me to do? To whom do I need to present the gospel? By sheer determination, I purpose to labor for You.

Because the Spirit of the Lord is in me, He can work through me to touch others with help, hope, and healing.

Action Point:

- On this day, I listen for the voice of the Lord (see Jeremiah 42:4-6).
- On this day, I am of good cheer (see John 16:33).
- On this day, I keep my eyes fixed on the Author and Finisher of my faith (see Hebrews 12:2).
- On this day, I walk uprightly (see Psalm 84:11).
- On this day, I invite Jesus into every interaction so that He can establish the work of my hands (see Psalm 90:17).

Hallelujah!

LOYALTY

Let every soul be subject to the governing authorities. For there is no authority except from God, and the authorities that exist are appointed by God. Therefore whoever resists the authority resists the ordinance of God, and those who resist will bring judgment on themselves.

ROMANS 13:1-2

Loyalty is one of those corporate buzzwords that people throw around at the office to make themselves sound as if they are above reproach. It's a word company leaders use when they are trying to keep the rank and file under control. It's a word employees use when they want better wages and improved working conditions.

As a Christian, my first loyalty is to God. He has ordained me to be where I am, right here, right now. Until I learn all He wants to teach me here and until I finish all He wants me to accomplish here, I'm not going anywhere.

My second loyalty, whether I like it or not, is to my governing authority: my boss, my supervisor, my department head. He may be a total jerk, but according to the Word of God, I am subject to him. She may be a total Jezebel, but according to the Word of God, I am subject to her. If I refuse to submit myself to authority as God requires, I am rebelling against God and His ordained order for my professional life.

Lord, You know when my loyalty to man may compromise my loyalty to You. In such cases I believe You will empower me to stand on Your Word and remain faithful to You. In all other circumstances I will submit to the authorities You have placed over me.

Action Point: Today I respectfully submit to my superiors.

CONSECRATION

Now it came to pass, when Moses had finished setting up the taber-
nacle, that he anointed it and sanctified it and all its furnishings,
and the altar and all its utensils; so he anointed them and sancti-
fied them.

NUMBERS 7:1

Lord, You have given me all that I have. I'm sorry that at times I forget it all belongs to You. In truth, if it weren't for You, I would have nothing, I would be nothing. So today I dedicate all that I have to You, the one, true living God, and I consecrate it for Your use.

Anointed by the power of the Holy Spirit, appointed by the might of the Most High God, let me strive to be consecrated and set apart for Your good works, doing what is necessary to be a vessel of honor fit for the Master's use (see 2 Timothy 2:21). Lord, I want the cup of my life to be clean through and through, so I dedicate myself to You, knowing that You can wash me and fill my cup till it overflows (see Psalm 23:5 and Luke 11:39). I want the blessing of a clean conscience so I can daily walk in a way that pleases You, doing what is right and standing in the light.

I give back to You, Lord, everything that You have blessed me with, knowing that Your gift to me will be a life that causes others to marvel because the hand of God has touched it.

Action Point:

- Today I dedicate this tabernacle I call "home" to You.
- Today I dedicate this tabernacle I call "myself" to You.
- Today I dedicate all that I have—my time, my talents, my heart, and my soul—to You.

STRESS

And let us not grow weary while doing good, for in due season we shall reap if we do not lose heart. Therefore, as we have opportunity, let us do good to all, especially to those who are of the household of faith.

GALATIANS 6:9-10

What a word Galatians has for me, especially now when I am stressed out and tired of giving my all. It seems that every day someone is in need, and I must perform some good deed. The Lord knows that I don't mind, but at times I wonder, *What about me?* I need attention, I need care, and truth be known, I need another person's prayers. Yet, when I feel uptight and stressed out, I look to God to pull me out, "not by might nor by power, but by [His] Spirit" (Zechariah 4:6). I continue to wait upon the Lord, for I delight in Him. He will renew my strength and give me flight (see Isaiah 40:31).

Today, no matter what may come my way, I will choose not to get stressed out. Instead, I will walk by faith and not by sight, for it is in God that I live and breathe and have my being (see Acts 17:28). So what do I *really* have to worry about? Why should I fret? I need only speak the name of the One who is greater than all the rest. "Jesus" is the sweetest name I know, and it is He who causes me to glow with love, patience, endurance, and inner peace. My love for God is the greatest antidote to stress. Thank You, Lord, for anointing me this day. Let me never grow weary of doing good, I pray.

Action Point: Today as stress knocks on the door of my heart, I call out to Jesus and open the door only to Him.

ENJOY the Fruits of Your Labor

You did not choose Me, but I chose you and appointed you that you should go and bear fruit, and that your fruit should remain, that whatever you ask the Father in My name He may give you.

John 15:16

Navigating the route to success can sometimes be like going through a maze blindfolded. In that maze you will encounter every detour, every booby trap, and every distraction imaginable. Our enemy has placed these roadblocks in our way to tempt us to sin, and his strategy works. We all stumble and fall, so it's not unusual to find ourselves trapped by wrong choices. We buy into satan's lies that the tempting fruit he offers is okay to bite into. Remember that sometimes, with that one bite, the good godly fruit of our labor goes bad.

Loving the World

Do not love the world or the things in the world. If anyone loves the world, the love of the Father is not in him. For all that is in the world—the lust of the flesh, the lust of the eyes, and the pride of life—is not of the Father but is of the world. And the world is passing away, and the lust of it; but he who does the will of God abides forever. (1 John 2:15-17)

So there you have it. All that the carnal man desires in the world falls into one of three categories:

- lust of the flesh
- lust of the eyes
- pride of life

As we train ourselves to look through our spiritual eyes by standing on the Word and spending regular time in prayer, we will get better at heeding the warning signs and better at *running* back to the Father. Our spiritual alert system will ever more quickly scream: "Setup! Setup!" Consider how these saboteurs present themselves in daily life and can compromise our ethics on the job:

Lust of the Flesh: weaknesses that have anything to do with food, fantasy, or feelings.

- *I have no idea how I've gained so much weight. Do you think fifty pounds in two months is bad? Lunch from twelve to two? No problem.*
- *I can't stop thinking about this gorgeous man at work. I know he's married, but we meet at the copy machine every chance we get. Flirting doesn't hurt a soul.*
- *I get so angry with my boss trying to tell me what to do. Who does she think she is? I'm going to work just enough to get by because the check doesn't change.*

Lust of the Eyes: temptations that are primarily materialistic.

- *I know we should be more accurate about our annual report, but it's okay to be optimistic for the sake of our investors.*
- *Listen, if I'm fortunate enough to know ahead of time that the stock is going to tumble, what's the problem? I have a wife and kids to feed, not to mention that huge mortgage.*

- *He should get the job simply because he looks the part—and he belongs to the country club my family has been a part of for years.*

Pride of Life: temptations that move us to think less of God and more of ourselves.

- *I know God's Word clearly states that I should give a tenth of my income, but that's my hard-earned money! Besides, I'm a generous giver.*
- *I want to be a good steward over the money God has given me. That's why I decided to invest in a Gentlemen's Club (a.k.a. a strip joint). Now, there's a business that's booming!*
- *Our debt is mounting monthly, and we can hardly make it, but I need that BMW to give my clients confidence in my ability to succeed.*

TIMELESS TEMPTATIONS

So when the woman saw that the tree was *good for food,* that it was *pleasant to the eyes,* and a tree *desirable to make one wise,* she took of its fruit and ate. She also gave to her husband with her, and he ate. (Genesis 3:6, emphasis added)

Lust and pride blur the lines in the sands of ethics, values, and conduct. When people say, "Things are so bad these days," remember that there is nothing new under the sun. And if you think that phrase was coined by some hip trendsetter of his time, check this out: "That which has been is what will be, that which is done is what will be done, and there is nothing new under the sun. Is there anything of which it may be said, 'See, this is new'? It has already been in ancient times before us" (Ecclesiastes 1:9-10).

Well, those ancient times bear proof that the devil then is the same devil now. The lust of the flesh, the lust of the eyes, and the pride of life are the very same temptations that the serpent used successfully in the Garden of Eden to lure Eve and Adam away from God and His perfect plan for them and the world.

The devil's trio of temptations is the same trio he used on Jesus after the Spirit of the Lord led Him into the wilderness to be tempted. Jesus had been praying and fasting for forty days.

Now when the tempter came to Him, he said, "If You are the Son of God, command that these stones become bread." [Here is lust of the flesh: Jesus was tired and hungry.] But He answered and said, "It is written, 'Man shall not live by bread alone, but by every word that proceeds from the mouth of God.'

Then the devil took Him up into the holy city, set Him on the pinnacle of the temple, and said to Him, "If You are the Son of God, throw Yourself down. For it is written: 'He shall give His angels charge over you' and 'In their hands they shall bear you up, lest you dash your foot against a stone.'" [Here is pride of life: satan wanted Jesus to misuse His spiritual powers for His own glory.] Jesus said to him, "It is written again, 'You shall not tempt the LORD your God.'"

Again, the devil took Him up on an exceedingly high mountain, and showed Him all the kingdoms of the world and their glory. And he said to Him, "All these things I will give You if You will fall down and worship me." [Finally here is lust of the eyes: satan wanted Jesus to focus on possessions and power.] Then Jesus said to him, "Away with you, Satan! For it is written,

'You shall worship the LORD your God, and Him only you shall serve.'"

Then the devil left Him, and behold, angels came and ministered to Him. (Matthew 4:3-11)

How is it that satan was able to trick Adam and Eve, and why is it that he daily tries everything "under the sun" to tempt us now? Because temptations work! There is only one case in history where they didn't work, and that was with Jesus. The Son of God was tempted, but He never once yielded to sin. We, on the other hand, will sometimes see sin coming at us with a bright neon sign attached to it, but because we are trained to see the natural world rather than the spiritual world, we fail to recognize that our enemy is still using the same old tactics he used to get us the last time around.

The only way to successfully survive temptation is to do what Jesus did: Focus on the Word of God. Every time satan tempted Him, our Lord responded with "It is written." Every time the devil tried to up the ante, Jesus neither argued with him nor considered the offers. He simply fixed His mind on what God had to say about the situation.

We can do the same. When we are tempted by the lust of the flesh, the lust of the eyes, or the pride of life, let us:

- Bind our mind to the mind of Christ (see 1 Corinthians 2:15-16). Repeat these words in the face of temptation: "I have the mind of Christ." It's hard to think about the temptation and Jesus at the same time.

- Speak to temptation with the Word of God, refuting it with truth. Rejoice when the devil leaves you alone, and trust that angels will come down from heaven and minister to you just as they did to Jesus (see Matthew 4:11).

Live Life and Enjoy

> I know that nothing is better for them than to rejoice, and to
> do good in their lives, and also that every man should eat and
> drink and enjoy the good of all his labor—it is the gift of God.
> (Ecclesiastes 3:12-13)

I can hear you asking: "Let's see. Lust of the flesh, lust of the eyes,
pride of life—is there anything in this life left for me to enjoy?" Of
course there is. In fact, there's something far better—and that's the
whole point! Sin robs us of the very joy God intends for us to know.
Our heavenly Father wants us to take pleasure in *all* the good that He's
created. Blessings await us in an ever-flowing stream of good things as
we are faithful to obey Him. There's only one hitch: We have to dip
from the right stream: His stream. We have to live His way. If you're
wondering which stream is His, a good place to start is with the Ten
Commandments (see Exodus 20). If what you're about to enjoy
doesn't fall into any of those categories—you're probably fishing in the
right place!

God *wants* us to eat, drink, and be merry. But don't go blabbing all
over town that Andria Hall told you God said we can serve the Lord
and be a lush, too. That's not at all what I'm saying. I'm simply stating
that God wants to bless us with the good fruits of our labor and our
work, accomplished with the mind of Christ, so we'll be a blessing
to others.

- *Eat* (see 2 Thessalonians 3:10): Our work should provide
  us enough money to allow us to eat and to feed our families. The Word says, if you don't work, you don't eat.
- *Drink* (see Luke 10:7): Our ministry should allow us the
  opportunity to enter another's home where there is joy and

peace. Let us come and spread the gospel with good tidings. Let us eat and drink what is offered because it is good for us to break bread with others.

- *Be merry* (see Luke 15:23): The prodigal son returned home, hungry, broke, and broken. He had experienced all the world had to offer. Upon seeing him, his father was overjoyed! We, too, can rejoice when another believer is encouraged back into the faith by our walk at work.

God is our perfect example of the original worker. He is an eternal Creator. Can't you just see Him taking joy in the labor of creating? When He made the world, He had already created the heavens and the earth, but the earth was still nothing more than a big, dark, watery blob. Imagine God cracking His knuckles and getting to work. He outdid Himself every time He said, "Let there be!" (Genesis 1). By the time He was finished, He was just so excited about all He had created that He blessed it all with one word: "Good."

He will bless the work of our hands as well. We are to work *joyfully* as unto the Lord. And when we do true satisfaction is never far away.

Practical Application

Search me, O God, and know my heart;
Try me, and know my anxieties;
And see if there is any wicked way in me,
And lead me in the way everlasting. (Psalm 139:23-24)

- As you read this month's devotionals, ask God to use them and His Word to expose the places in your heart where the lust of the flesh, the lust of the eyes, and the pride of life make their home.

- As you discover these areas, confess them to God, then to your prayer partner or a godly counselor. Have him or her lift you up in prayer as you begin the tough job of rooting these areas out of your life to make room for the mind of Christ and the joy of the Lord.

Spiritual Truth

His lord said to him, "Well done, good and faithful servant; you have been faithful over a few things, I will make you ruler over many things. Enter into the joy of your lord." Matthew 25:23

Our faithful obedience to God in our labor will lead us to greater blessings and deeper joy.

Fifth Steps

- Give yourself permission to take pleasure both in the work God has set before you and in the fruit it yields.
- Confess your sins to God so that they won't inhibit God's purposes for your life or the joy you can have in your work.
- Strengthen your heart and mind against temptation by staying close to the Word.

Journal Exercises

Compare a day in which you experienced great joy in your work with a day in which joy seemed entirely out of reach. Explore the circumstances that influenced your feelings. Was your lack of joy the result of sin? Or did it elude you because you allowed external factors (such as someone else's wrongdoing) to rob you of joy? When your heart is joyful, is it because you have a firm hold of God's promises? Or does joy come only when your circumstances are good? Write down three ways in which you can begin to align your joy with the promises of God even when external factors threaten to take it away from you.

The Joy of the Lord Is My Strength

O Lord, You are to me a luscious fruit,
And I delight in Your sweet nectar.
My soul is hungry to do Your will,
And I desire to please Thee.
O Lord, Your Word to me is like crystal waters,
And I rejoice in having it wash over me,
Cleansing, purifying, and quenching the parched places
    of my soul.
O Lord, Your hand upholds me, and no matter what the
    day may bring,
Victory or defeat, I will still rejoice in this one thing:
Your strength is my joy, and my joy is to stand before You,
The perfect God, resting in this one truth:
You know and see far beyond mere circumstances
And peer deep into the heart of man.
So, Father, I pray that my walk before You is pure; that
    my work today
Will glorify You in every way;
That my words today will magnify You; and that my
    actions will

Shout to all those around me of the integrity that ought
      to be
Associated with a disciple of Jesus Christ, who is the
      Lord God Almighty!
Amen.

BOLDNESS

Now when they saw the boldness of Peter and John, and perceived that they were uneducated and untrained men, they marveled. And they realized that they had been with Jesus.

ACTS 4:13

I will never let someone else make me feel inferior or unequipped. I refuse to allow anyone's mind games to have power over my thoughts when it comes to the abilities, skills, or potential God has given me. I believe God has divinely placed me in this position and that only He can remove me. A few of the best minds in this place don't know the gospel, and because they don't know it, I must make myself available to God for the moment when He wants me to tell them of it. The Lord is interested in saving souls and glorifying His Son (see 2 Peter 3:9,18). Therefore, when God gives me an opportunity, I will be bold about my beliefs. I will daily be about my Father's business (see Luke 2:49).

"Now, Lord…grant to Your servants that with all boldness they may speak Your word…."
And when they had prayed, the place where they were assembled together was shaken; and they were all filled with the Holy Spirit, and they spoke the word of God with boldness. (Acts 4:29-31)

Even in the face of persecution and challenge, I willingly and joy-fully stand up as a soldier in the army of the Lord (see 2 Timothy 2:3). Father, I pray that others will know that I've been with Jesus.

Action Point: Today I look for opportunities to speak with wisdom the words that the Lord asks me to impart.

FAVOR

*Let not mercy and truth forsake you; bind them around your neck,
write them on the tablet of your heart, and so find favor and high
esteem in the sight of God and man.*

PROVERBS 3:3-4

Many times I've heard people say, "It's not what you know, but who you
know." They're right—and I know the Man in charge! I make every
effort to follow His rules, and the Word says if I do, He will give me
"favor and high esteem." When I maintain an attitude of mercy toward
others, when I stand for truth no matter what the price, God will
give me "favor and high esteem" in His sight and in the sight of my
colleagues.

We all face challenges in today's work environment, where we must
do more with less and sometimes without fair compensation. The reality is that cycles of hard times come and go. Hard times require me to
stand by faith in God's truth without compromise. In good times I will
remain committed to walk in His ways in spite of the world's many
attractive distractions.

Lord, daily remind me of Your standard for living. May my attitude
toward others be one of gratitude and compassion. Lord, etch this standard on the tablets of my heart. And if You see fit, grant me favor first
with You and then with all those who see my light shining. Let them
glorify You by what You've done in my life—and then let them believe.

Action Point: Today, as a symbolic act of writing God's commands
on the tablet of my heart, I write the following on a piece of paper and
post it in plain sight: "Let your heart keep my commands; for length of
days and long life and peace they will add to you" (Proverbs 3:1-2).

JOY

My brethren, count it all joy when you fall into various trials, knowing that the testing of your faith produces patience. But let patience have its perfect work, that you may be perfect and complete, lacking nothing.

JAMES 1:2-4

Lord, You really are going to have to work with me on this one. You want me to "count it *all* joy," but sometimes I see nothing joyful about my everyday circumstances. People here try my patience, situations challenge me beyond my limit, and the day-to-day stuff of working gets on my last nerve. Yet Your Word says that through it all I should find *joy*, not sadness, and *joy*, not madness, in these situations. That's because within every challenge is an opportunity. In every trial is a lesson that, if I learn it, will move me closer to completion in Christ. Through my trials, You are molding me and making me more like Your precious and perfect Son, Jesus. Under Your sovereignty, these trials have the power to transform my attitudes and remake my heart.

Patience is the key. When I *practice* patience, I am better equipped to assist others in their work and walk. When I *practice* patience, I am better able to wait on You. When I *practice* patience, I can withstand any assault and tackle daily challenges in a godly fashion appropriate for a Christian.

When I am being tried and tested on every front, I will remember to count it *all* joy, knowing that patience will have its perfect work in me. Ultimately I will experience the joy that You give as, by Your grace, I serve You.

Action Point: Today I choose to joyfully lean on You when the going gets rough and breathe deeply, too.

GENEROSITY

This service that you perform is not only supplying the needs of God's people but is also overflowing in many expressions of thanks to God. Because of the service by which you have proved yourselves, men will praise God for the obedience that accompanies your confession of the gospel of Christ, and for your generosity in sharing with them and with everyone else.

2 CORINTHIANS 9:12-13, NIV

Father, above all else, I want to bring praises to You. Too often I focus on my desire for You to supply *my* needs when, in fact, it is my Christian obligation to supply the needs of Your people. Your Word calls me to serve them and to generously share with them. That means I should perform my job duties with an open heart.

Today, Lord Jesus, it is my intent to not just show up for work, but to "show out" too! I will perform my tasks to the point of overflowing. As I do, I will inwardly praise You to the extreme! You tell me that when I do this it will prove to others by example that I am a follower of Christ. When obedience accompanies my confession, others can see my walk and glorify You.

Action Point:

- Help me this day, Holy Spirit, to open up my heart with generosity toward others.
- Help me this day, Holy Spirit, to keep my mind focused on serving God's people.
- Help me this day, Holy Spirit, to share with others my time and talent so that I might glorify Jesus with a generous heart.

TRUST

But let all those rejoice who put their trust in You; let them ever shout for joy, because You defend them; let those also who love Your name Be joyful in You. For You, O LORD, will bless the righteous; with favor You will surround him as with a shield.

PSALM 5:11-12

Father God, I want to be someone whom people look at and say, "Why is she so happy all the time?" I want to be a person who always puts my trust in You. I know that trusting You goes against conventional wisdom, and it certainly runs an opposite course to what man would think, but the truth of the matter is that I can't put my trust anywhere *but* in You. Life's circumstances change like the shifting wind. Today there is "security"; tomorrow there is uncertainty. What is sure and what is true? Is my employment really ever a sure thing? Is my coming paycheck a rock-solid certainty? Will the emergency money I have stashed away be enough to sustain me? Certainly not, but You, O Lord, are my Source. You, dear Jesus, are my Salvation. You are my Provider and my Shield.

Long after I leave this workplace, long after my colleagues have come and gone, long after this present situation is a distant memory, You will still be here. If I don't learn to put my total trust in You, then I will make myself vulnerable and exposed. Father God, I ask that You gently remind me to trust You, to put my joy in You, and to walk righteously so that I can bask in the favor You give and be protected by the shield You provide.

Action Point: Today I praise God for His trustworthiness in the midst of the world's uncertainties.

REJOICE

I know that nothing is better for them than to rejoice, and to do good in their lives, and also that every man should eat and drink and enjoy the good of all his labor—it is the gift of God.

ECCLESIASTES 3:12-13

When I rejoice in the work God has given me to do for Him, even if I'm less than pleased, I find a joy within my heart that will never really leave. This joy is a precious gift from God.

When I make rejoicing a habit for my life, I know God will enable me to flee from stress and strife. When I rejoice in the good and refuse to give authority to the bad, that moment of decision reminds me of the blessings that I have.

Right now I decide to celebrate the work and labor of my hands. I will revel in God's goodness and rejoice in His perfect plan. I exult and I delight. I am thankful day and night. I accept the good gifts from God above. I am ever grateful for His precious gifts and life-sustaining love.

Action Point: Today I rejoice in the work God has given me to do.

EDIFICATION

He Himself gave some to be apostles, some prophets, some evangelists, and some pastors and teachers.

EPHESIANS 4:11

Father God, am I blessed as an apostle, prophet, evangelist, pastor, or teacher? What marvelous gift have You given me—and why?

...for the equipping of the saints for the work of ministry,
for the edifying of the body of Christ... (verse 12)

Dear Lord Jesus, please show me how to use Your gifts in my workplace to equip Your people so that we might all be built-up.

...till we all come to the unity of the faith and of the knowledge of the Son of God, to a perfect man, to the measure
of the stature of the fullness of Christ... (verse 13)

I desire to measure up to "the stature of the fullness of Christ," but I see I can do this only when "we all come to the unity of the faith." Help me, Holy Spirit, to grasp fully the knowledge of the Son of God.

...that we should no longer be children, tossed to and fro
and carried about with every wind of doctrine... (verse 14)

Help me, Father, to *grow up spiritually* so that I am not easily influenced by the world, but am instead an influencer for Christ in the world. Show me, Lord, how to do my part and effectively work and not lose heart.

Action Point: Today I look for a way to use my spiritual gifts to edify a colleague lovingly and sensitively.

HAPPINESS

If a man has recently married, he must not be sent to war or have any other duty laid on him. For one year he is to be free to stay at home and bring happiness to the wife he has married.

DEUTERONOMY 24:5, NIV

Lord, You really got that one right! I can't imagine that work in Old Testament times would have been as stressful, as demanding, or as challenging as it is today. Yet back then it was law that family life should take precedence over work for a period of time. Imagine being told as a newlywed, "Stay home for at least one year because God wants you to focus on one thing: Figure out how to make each other happy."

Even for newlyweds, happiness is not something that just happens. It must be nurtured. It must be cultivated. And apparently, Lord, you think enough of my happiness to command me, in principle at least, to carve out time to cultivate joy. Whether married or single, I pray for balance and for time to nurture my heart. Lord, I may not have a complete year without distraction. I may not have a wife or husband with whom I can cultivate this happiness. Even so, Father, I realize that joy is not something to be hoarded, but shared. I am free to extend Your happiness to those close to me. Lord, may my extension of happiness to my relationships be pleasing in Your sight and bring a smile to Your face.

Action Point: Today I share whatever happiness I experience with at least one other person.

PRIVILEGE

Out of the most severe trial, their overflowing joy and their extreme poverty welled up in rich generosity. For I testify that they gave as much as they were able, and even beyond their ability. Entirely on their own, they urgently pleaded with us for the privilege of sharing in this service to the saints. And they did not do as we expected, but they gave themselves first to the Lord and then to us in keeping with God's will.

2 CORINTHIANS 8:2-5, NIV

Lord, it is a great privilege to share with others the spiritual life You have given me. I want to create in my work environment a place where I can openly express who I am in Christ—by my actions and, when appropriate, my words. I want the work I do to speak spiritual volumes of what it means to be a follower of Christ so that others will want to know You. I want to bear fruit that is fitting for one who is changed daily by faith in the living God. "But the fruit of the Spirit is love, joy, peace, longsuffering, kindness, goodness, faithfulness, gentleness, self-control" (Galatians 5:22-23). In Jesus, I have no limitations. In Him, I have no lack. Because of the Spirit at work in me, I am rich in love, patience, talent, wisdom, and faith.

How can I share daily what I have with others? What can I do today that will exemplify my faith in action and, through that action, bring glory to God? Whether You, Father, would have me give of my time, my skill, my joy, or my assistance, please increase my ability so that I can extend this great privilege into the realm of infinite possibility. When I allow Your Holy Spirit to work through me, I can be of great service.

Action Point: Today I joyfully and willingly put my life at Your service.

REPLENISHMENT

"The LORD bless you, O home of justice, and mountain of holiness!" And there shall dwell in Judah itself, and in all its cities together, farmers and those going out with flocks. For I have satiated the weary soul, and I have replenished every sorrowful soul.

JEREMIAH 31:23-25

The Word of the Lord is an encouragement to my weary soul. It extends a promise of better days to come. I will guard my mind as a home of justice, my soul as a "mountain of holiness."

Every day, the temptation to criticize and complain sets itself before me. When I give in, I influence my coworkers to eat the "nothing is ever right; no one is good enough" sour grapes that set their teeth on edge. If the devil had his way, a spirit of dissatisfaction would overtake my place of employment. A root of bitterness would take firm hold.

I will not allow the enemy to use me. I will counter his attacks with joy and love. But I must equip myself for battle by going to God for replenishment. When I am heavy laden, I know Jesus will give me rest (see Matthew 11:28). Like a farmer, I want to sow seeds that will bear good fruit. Like a shepherd, I want to protect my flock. In both cases, I want to make the most of every opportunity by offering refreshment to those who are in need. People who mind what they say and do are a refreshment to others. I long to be such a person.

God, please use me as a vessel to water my colleagues with a word of refreshment and warm them with a word of hope.

Action Point: Today I resist the temptation to criticize or complain, and I look to God for strength as I seek to counter any negative spirits present in the workplace.

MORALE

But the following night the Lord stood by him and said, "Be of good cheer, Paul; for as you have testified for Me in Jerusalem, so you must also bear witness at Rome."

ACTS 23:11

What a blessing to know that my God will stand by me even in the darkest of times. Just as the Lord stood by Paul and encouraged him with a word of what he must do, God encourages me to stand and bear witness of His mercy, His goodness, His peace, and His protection. Today just might be the day to let someone else know that God is far better than an afternoon cup of coffee. Jesus Christ is the greatest pick-me-up, and it is in Him that I find my joy. When others around me are busy complaining about their workload, their coworkers, their bosses, or their paychecks, I will instead exalt the Most High God and place my trust in Him.

"Be exalted, O LORD, in Your own strength! We will sing and praise Your power" (Psalm 21:13). Lord, I will sing because You have given me a precious song of faith. I will praise You, for in Your power I can rejoice. Today I choose to maintain an attitude of gratitude. If the mood in my office is less than joyful, then use me, Father, as an agent for change.

Action Point: Today I set the morale barometer in my workplace by bringing the encouragement offered by God-given peace, love, happiness, and joy. May it be sincere—not merely optimistic—rooted in Truth, and as contagious as a corporate cold!

GRATITUDE

We give thanks to you, O God, we give thanks, for your Name is near; men tell of your wonderful deeds.

PSALM 75:1, NIV

When I think of all that I have to be grateful for, I don't have time to sit around and gossip. When I acknowledge the goodness and mercy of God, I won't waste words speaking about things that don't matter. When I part my lips to lift up the name of the Lord, all I want to do is tell everyone of His wonderful works in my life.

So right now, I am going to express to You, O God, my gratitude for all You have given me this day. I am grateful for breath. I am grateful for life. I am grateful to have a job. I am grateful for the chance to positively impact others. I am grateful for my salvation. I am grateful for Your saving grace. I am grateful to have religious freedom. I am grateful for my liberty in Christ. I am grateful for my daily bread. I am grateful for Your forgiveness.

I am grateful, Lord, for *everything*. I am grateful because You have called me to be Yours. I am grateful that I am Your "workmanship, created in Christ Jesus for good works, which [You] prepared beforehand, that [I] should walk in them" (Ephesians 2:10). So, Father, as I give thanks to You, I remember Your loving-kindness. May I never take for granted the life You have bestowed upon me. Continue to reveal Your plans for me, plans that will glorify You in every way, every day. Lord, I am so very grateful!

Action Point: Today I thank God for the joy He gives me, the joy that helps me endure any circumstance.

HEART

Jesus said to him, " 'You shall love the LORD your God with all your heart, with all your soul, and with all your mind.' This is the first and great commandment."

MATTHEW 22:37-38

Many people will say of someone who has the courage to take a stand, "Boy, that one sure has a lot of heart." Perhaps this remark comes because so few people are really willing to speak up for their convictions. For Christians, however, "having a lot of heart" is not just about being courageous. It's about following a commandment: "Love the Lord your God with all your heart."

Love is the greatest offering I can give to God. Far greater than my need for Him, far beyond my belief in Him, the love I have for my Father in heaven should be so all-encompassing that I can express it fully with all my heart, soul, and mind.

That pretty much sums it up! Jesus said in John 14:15, "If you love Me, keep My commandments." That should tell me something about the kind of love God is looking for. He wants me to demonstrate my love for Him through my obedience. David cries out in Psalm 42:2, "My soul thirsts for God." My soul should long for the Lord as if I were parched and dry and desperate for water. Paul writes in 1 Corinthians 2:16, "But we have the mind of Christ." And so my mind should be fixed on Jesus.

Lord, I want to truly love You according to Your definition, not mine. When people see me, may I give them reason to say, "That one sure has a lot of heart!" and know that my heart thirsts for You (see Psalm 42:2).

Action Point: Today I ask God to fill me with the kind of love of which He alone is worthy.

INTEGRITY

He who is faithful in what is least is faithful also in much; and he who is unjust in what is least is unjust also in much.... And if you have not been faithful in what is another man's, who will give you what is your own?

LUKE 16:10,12

Many times have I thought to myself, *I could run my own business.* Many ideas have come to mind of which I've said, "I could do that." And in my professional career, I have worked for many people and declared, "I'm just as talented as they are!"

Well, in such cases what I say is not as important as what I do. Even when there's no one else around to monitor my work, God is looking at my actions every second of the day. My professional integrity should be just as important to me as fulfilling my personal dreams. It is critical in God's eyes that I do what I say and follow through with my daily responsibilities.

God says that when I prove faithful with little I will also prove faithful with much, and He will bless me accordingly: "For to everyone who has, more will be given, and he will have abundance" (Matthew 25:29). Similarly, if I am unfair even in small dealings, certainly I will be unfair in larger matters too, but when I stand as a trustworthy steward, when I remain faithful to Him, He will be the One to give me my reward (see Colossians 3:24).

Action Point: Today I labor as though God Himself were sharing an office with me.

JESUS

Therefore God also has highly exalted Him and given Him the name which is above every name, that at the name of Jesus every knee should bow...and that every tongue should confess that Jesus Christ is Lord, to the glory of God the Father.

PHILIPPIANS 2:9-11

Lord, why is it that people who don't know You get so freaked out at the mention of Your name? Maybe I used to be one of those people.

I want to ask Your forgiveness: There was a time when I didn't fully understand just how important Your name is—perhaps I still don't fully understand. Fearing the offense of others, I hold back my praise of You. My mouth doesn't always speak Your name not because I'm ashamed, but because at times it seems easier to talk "generally" about God.

But starting today, I will no longer relegate You to a whisper in my prayers. Starting today I will bring You out of my closet and—if the Holy Spirit leads—into the conference room. I don't have to bash people over the head with my faith in You, but I should hold my own head high when I reverently mention Your name: Jesus.

Whether in casual conversation or in someone's pointed investigation of my beliefs, I am ready to call out and call upon the only name that can save me. The only name that is above all other names. The only name that will bring glory to the Father. That name is Jesus, and I am honored to call on You this day!

Action Point: Today I ask the Holy Spirit for assistance in quashing the fears, shame, anxieties, and cowardliness that prevent me from proclaiming the powerful, awesome, magnificent name of Jesus.

LIBERTY

Now the Lord is the Spirit; and where the Spirit of the Lord is, there is liberty.

2 CORINTHIANS 3:17

T.G.I.M.? Normally all of us at the office think T.G.I.F.: *Thank God It's Friday!* Today I'm going to switch that, not just from my mouth, but from my heart. "Thank God It's Monday!" That's right. I'm taking the liberty I have as a believer in Christ to invite the Holy Spirit into my office, into my work, and wherever He might decide to use me this day. For "where the Spirit of the Lord is, there is liberty."

- Thank God it's Monday and I have a job to go to.
- Thank God it's Monday and I know Jesus.
- Thank God it's Monday and the sun still rises in the east.
- Thank God it's Monday and I have breath in my body.
- Thank God it's Monday and the ocean still ebbs and flows.
- Thank God it's Monday and I have a smile on my face, because yesterday was Sunday, and I'm a recipient of God's great grace!
- Thank God it's Monday!
- Thank God tomorrow is Tuesday…
- And the next day is Wednesday…

I have the liberty to thank God for today because His mercies are new every morning.

Action Point: Today I thank God for the liberty He gives me. This day I rejoice in the freedom I have to believe!

"Making It Big"

Rest in the LORD, and wait patiently for Him; do not fret because of him who prospers in his way, because of the man who brings wicked schemes to pass.

PSALM 37:7

Do I really want to be defined by others as that person who is "making it big"? Oftentimes, making it big comes with an equally big price tag that I may not be willing to pay. I can look around and see others who have a better position, a better house, a better car...but I don't know what they had to *give* up in order to *get* these things.

Did they give up their time? Did they give up their marriage? Did they give up their relationship with You? Did they sell somebody else down the river in order to sail on smooth waters? Did they step on the back of another to get farther up the ladder? I don't know!

God, when I worry or fret over the prosperity of others, check my spirit. Maybe they've truly been a good steward and You've chosen to bless them. If so, praise Your holy name. Maybe they've prospered by bringing wicked schemes to pass. In either case, You alone will judge all things. For You cause the sun to rise on the evil and the good, and You send "rain on the just and on the unjust" (Matthew 5:45).

I want to "make it," yes, but only according to Your yardstick, not by the world's measure. Cleanse my heart, Lord. Take away any feelings of envy I might have toward others who seem to be doing better than I am. I don't have to worry about how they made it. Such preoccupation only takes my eyes off You.

Action Point: Today I rest in God's mysterious ways and wait patiently for Him to reveal the blessings He has in store for me.

MISERY

But since you are like lukewarm water, I will spit you out of my mouth! You say, "I am rich. I have everything I want. I don't need a thing!" And you don't realize that you are wretched and miserable and poor and blind and naked.

REVELATION 3:16-17, NLT

So many people walk around being miserable. They never have anything good to say. They're always sullen and wry. They never seem to have any joy at all. Perhaps at times I've been that way too.

Being miserable is a choice. Worse yet, it is a sin because misery defies our need for Christ! God warns that those of us who are dishonest about our true state will never enter the kingdom of heaven. Pride is at the heart of misery. Pride is what got satan kicked out of heaven in the first place (see Isaiah 14:12-14). It is easy to reach a point in life where we believe we don't need a thing. We become puffed up with the car, with the career, with the house. We make ourselves the masters of our fate, and when all is said and sung, we announce, "I did it my way!" We don't even realize we are pitiful and deprived and blind and unprotected.

Lord, please expose whatever misery I harbor for the pride that it is. Without Christ we are all wretched! Without Christ we are all poor! Without Christ we are all blind! Without Christ we are all unprotected! And yet all we have to do to cast off our misery is acknowledge our true condition and then rejoice because we've found You.

Action Point: Today, if I see people who are miserable, I lift them up in prayer. Lord, help me to lessen their despair by shining Your light of hope on their lives. Please give me opportunity to tell them of the living Savior who can bring them joy once more.

OBSERVATION

The heavens declare the glory of God; the skies proclaim the work of his hands.

PSALM 19:1, NIV

God is good—and so is His creation! I need to go outside more to observe nature so I, too, can proclaim, "It is good!"

When I turn my heart toward God to see His glory all around me, I am more grateful, I am more settled, I am more delighted. The seemingly small things that I take for granted often have the power to remind me that *God is.* The ocean clearly cries out with its crashing waves—*God is!* The sky, simply magnificent in splendid sunlight or ominous gloom, is evidence of His mighty hand. My life, my very breath, shows me that God is an awesome Architect who knows all about me: Every hair is counted (see Matthew 10:30), and every intimate detail was crafted before time.

Lord, please strengthen my powers of observation. Help me to see Your handiwork that others might not notice, and give me opportunity to share the delight of my discovery. Help me to hear the voice of Your creation: "Day after day they pour forth speech; night after night they display knowledge" (Psalm 19:2, NIV). May it speak to me of Your sovereignty and majesty.

Action Point: Today is the day that You have made. I rejoice and am glad in it (see Psalm 118:24). I marvel in joyfully observing the divine in all its detail.

PRAISE

The LORD is my strength and song, and He has become my salvation; He is my God, and I will praise Him.

EXODUS 15:2

On some days, work is nothing to sing about. It's difficult, frustrating, or so utterly unsatisfying that singing Your praise becomes the last thing on my mind and the furthest thing from my lips. Those days, however, are the best times for me to take a moment, relax, and *breeeeathe* in this thought: *The Lord is my strength and song.*

Now, what does that mean? *He is my strength* means that I don't have to be a tower or a testimony every moment to those around me. I don't always have to be the go-to guy. I don't have to despair when I fall—into boredom, depression, anxiety, or sin—because I know that my God will never leave me and that His hand is mighty to save.

He is my song means I can find joy in Him. He alone is worthy of the praise and enthusiasm of my victorious voice. There is only one song for me to sing, and that song is *the Lord.*

He has become my salvation means Jesus came to save *me!* Now, this concept is hard to grasp: The Son of God loves me so deeply, so completely, that He left His throne above and came to earth. His strength is indeed great enough to save, and by His sacrifice at Calvary, He did exactly that. So I sing because God in His mercy and strength saw fit to save me: "You are my God. You are my King. How could I not praise You? Forever and ever, Amen."

Action Point: Lord, today I let loose the joy I've found in the saving power of Your strength, and I praise You for it with all my might.

SURRENDER Everything to Christ

During the days of Jesus' life on earth, he offered up prayers and petitions with loud cries and tears to the one who could save him from death, and he was heard because of his reverent submission.

HEBREWS 5:7, NIV

No one starts out looking at success from God's perspective. Instead of looking upward, we either turn inward or to the world to define *ultimate success*—and then we *go for it!* We go for the education. We go for the job. We go for the career. We go for the money. We go for the car. We go for the big house. We go for the gusto! And after we've gone and gone and gone, we finally realize that we're going nowhere fast. When all is said and done, every cliché that you can think of holds true.

- All that glitters is not gold.
- Money can't buy you happiness or love.
- Without your health and strength you have nothing.

So what is *success?* And how do we achieve it without losing our peace, losing ourselves, losing our souls? No one sets out to fail at any endeavor. And yet too many of us for too long seek after the things of this world instead of the things of God. We spend a lifetime striving to attain the temporal instead of the eternal. When we've traveled the road to achievement only to learn that *true* success cannot be found in status or wealth, God's perspective, as revealed to us in His Word, is the only one that makes sense.

The Back-Road Route to Success

> Because the foolishness of God is wiser than men, and the weakness of God is stronger than men. (1 Corinthians 1:25)

Look up the word *success* in the dictionary, and you'll find many things we should strive for: achievement, triumph, conquest. However, when you come across the antonym of these words, you'll find one term: *surrender.* As with many of God's principles, taking the path to success through surrender might seem backward in the eyes of the world. But that path is the only one that will get us there.

I was once privileged to be used by God as a conduit for a very good friend of mine. I'll call her Kelsi. I helped her get a job with an international nonprofit agency. The job's promises were tantalizing, but shortly after she started working, a management change brought an unexpected storm of professional trials. Many of us have been in Kelsi's shoes. In today's corporate environment of layoffs, downsizing, and managerial maneuvering, a typical storm might look like hers:

- *Changes in Corporate Structure.* First Kelsi reported directly to the president. When the company added a management layer, she received a different supervisor.
- *Redesignation of Office Space.* Kelsi originally had her own office and a fair amount of autonomy. When the new manager redesigned the office space, Kelsi had a less functional space half the size of what she had been used to.

- *Micromanagement and Scrutiny.* Under the new management, Kelsi's initiative and ideas were second-guessed and scrutinized despite her successful track record.

In circumstances like these, God is trying to get your attention. He'll allow the circumstances of your life to squeeze you until you cry out to Him at every turn. As if Kelsi's workplace issues weren't causing her enough stress, my dear friend was simultaneously bombarded with extreme personal challenges:

- a dying parent who lived more than three hundred miles away—and Kelsi is an only child
- a husband out of work on Wall Street, a casualty of 9/11
- one son in college who lives at home and another son approaching the teenage years with all that busyness and hormonal drama
- mounting bills
- the death of a beloved dog

My friend, the original Ms. Fix-It, couldn't fix this. My precious sister in Christ, the ultimate multitasker, the accomplished problem solver, who by nature has something of a controlling personality, was deep into problems that could only be solved by the Lord. Kelsi and I prayed together, fasted, and talked things through. She finally decided to surrender any and all of her perceived control to Him. She began to assess the real priorities in her life. Despite all that was going on at work, she knew she had to focus on what was truly important.

Through it all, I witnessed Kelsi's relationship with and dependence on the Lord grow deeply and sweetly into an abiding and intimate relationship with Him. Her attitude toward her troubles was transformed. Of work she now says, "No matter how much they tried to box me in and alienate me, what they didn't know was that I was only able to stand because I was standing with a mighty God. Only on His timetable—not theirs and not mine—would my testing be over. This was a test in patience, tolerance, and true surrender."

Oh, if we would all desire to grow toward that place where nothing else matters but Jesus Christ. That's where Kelsi is now. I'm sure that's where she'll stay. "When others began to take credit for my work, it just didn't matter," she says, looking back. "When colleagues I had mentored and promoted stabbed me in the back, it just didn't matter. What *did* matter was that I was standing with God—focusing on the bigger picture and what He was trying to accomplish in my life. In order to receive that, I had to enter into the process of total and complete surrender to Him." Surrender, however, is a lifelong process.

I SURRENDER ALL

> Therefore submit to God. Resist the devil and he will flee from
> you. Draw near to God and He will draw near to you. Cleanse
> your hands, you sinners; and purify your hearts, you double-
> minded. (James 4:7-8)

What does a surrendered life look like? What are some practical ways we can submit to God? Another word for submission is humility, which is the inner acknowledgment of how **BIG** God is and how small we really are. Humility is a personality trait that must be cultivated by the Spirit of God, who can help us realize our dependence on Him.

David had a humble heart and a submissive attitude toward God. We must pray for a spirit like David's.

> Lord, make me to know my end,
> And what is the measure of my days,

That I may know how frail I am.

Indeed, You have made my days as handbreadths,

And my age is as nothing before You;

Certainly every man at his best state is but vapor. Selah.

Surely every man walks about like a shadow;

Surely they busy themselves in vain;

He heaps up riches,

And does not know who will gather them. (Psalm 39:4-6)

If we want to walk in the power of the Lord, if we want to be effective Christians in the workplace, we must say as John the Baptist did, "He must increase, but I must decrease" (John 3:30). Decreasing means:

- seeking God's will, not ours, in all circumstances,
- reading and studying God's Word to gain His perspective on all situations, and
- obeying His direction for our lives even if it means being singled out for our beliefs.

A big part of surrendering means placing your trust completely in the Lord. Build upon your faith of the past and divest yourself of any particular desired outcome for any specific situation. In other words, don't be attached to what it is you want, but do stay close to your Source and what He wants. God is keenly aware of what roadblocks lie ahead as well as what blessings He has down the road for you. God knows all things and sees all things.

The alternative to surrender to God is not success, but empty striving. You can avoid the kind of wandering in the desert for years that the headstrong Israelites did by submitting to God's authority and inviting God to take over your life. A word of caution, though: When you say, "Jesus, take over the reins of my life, including my professional life," you'd better buckle up. I guarantee that you'll end up somewhere you never thought you'd be, doing something you never thought you could, and being used by Him in ways that you truly know you are incapable of doing on your own.

Monday *is* going to roll around, and we all will head back to work. We could view it as "another day, another dollar." Or we can shift our perspective and look at work as "another day, another miracle." When we change the way we think about our jobs, we free the Holy Spirit to work through us, in us, and around us. Our lives are enriched, and others examine our walk and wonder: *How can I get some of that?* Our walk at work will be most effective when we apply spiritual principles not just in crisis but to our daily routine.

LET THE SEASONS CHANGE

> To everything there is a season,
> A time for every purpose under heaven. (Ecclesiastes 3:1)

As I shared in chapter 1, my job at CNN was a real gift from God; it was my "Midnight-Hour Miracle." I have no question that the Lord placed me there. It was a tremendous blessing in my life and, I believe, in the lives of others as well. All along, my "work" at CNN was never *just* to deliver the news. Many of my coworkers would come to me and whisper, "Andria, I see you are a Christian, and I know that you pray. Will you please pray for my mother—she's dying; my sister—she has breast cancer; my wife—she lost her job; my state board exams—I'm not sure I'll pass…" That blessing, however, became a testing ground for my faith.

For nearly two years I commuted to CNN's offices in Atlanta from New Jersey and worked four days a week. Every Saturday and Sunday afternoon I would begin my evening newscasts the same way: "Live—from the CNN Center in Atlanta. I'm Andria Hall and this is *World*

View." What prestige, what privilege. Every Monday morning I would take the first flight out of Hartsfield International Airport back into Newark and then return home to an even greater privilege: being with my husband and three children for three days.

At first, I was thrilled—and spiritually innocent. And boy oh boy did the Lord grant me favor! I praise God's holy name for how He took care of me and my family during that back-and-forth craziness. Living apart from my family afforded us many career and financial opportunities and certainly took me several rungs up the ladder of worldly success. But after a while I realized that the separation was an unhealthy temptation and a formula for disaster.

God may choose to separate us from those we love for a season. That's what He did in my life. That's what He has done from the very beginning. Think back to Abram: "Now the LORD had said to Abram: 'Get out of your country, from your family and from your father's house, to a land that I will show you. I will make you a great nation; I will bless you and make your name great; and you shall be a blessing. I will bless those who bless you, and I will curse him who curses you; and in you all the families of the earth shall be blessed" (Genesis 12:1-3).

Well, it's a long story, but during his journey away from home, Abram ended up in a place called Sodom and Gomorrah. The Bible says, "The men of Sodom were exceedingly wicked and sinful against the LORD" (Genesis 13:13). For me, I eventually came to a place where I could see clearly that my life away from my family was leading to sin because our lives were truly "out of order."

There I was, a wife and mother leading a parallel life as jetsetter and part-time single. My husband was alone in New Jersey, working in the Big Apple, doing double Daddy duty because I was not there. And I was not altogether *bad looking.* And he is, if I may say so, not all together *bad looking.* Not a good combination for a healthy and happy family life.

I finally recognized that my season for being at CNN was coming to a close when, one evening as I headed out the door for Atlanta, the scene in my home looked something like this: *I'm in my standard travel uniform—all black. Black slacks, black sweater, black heels. My youngest son, seven at the time, never looks up from the television to say good-bye. My daughter, twelve at the time, yells from upstairs, "See you, Mom." No hug, no kiss. My husband is quiet, the way he's pretty much been the entire time I was home. And my middle son, ten at the time, is on the floor, holding on to my pants leg and crying, "Mommy, please don't go. Don't go."*

The winds of change had shifted. My life could either end up in Sodom and Gomorrah, or I could get on my knees, ask for forgiveness for not seeing things as they were sooner, and pray to be released from my assignment at CNN. In a word, I needed to surrender to God's perfect order.

God's Perfect Order

> He who finds his life will lose it, and he who loses his life for My sake will find it. (Matthew 10:39)

I believe that because I surrendered to God, He graciously orchestrated my departure just as He had orchestrated my hire. I left Atlanta five months after my personal epiphany and came back home to be whom the Lord has called me to be: a servant to Him, a wife, a mother, and a business owner—yes, in that order. You see, evaluating where you are in your walk with God and whether you're on the right track requires you to line up your life with the order that He has established:

- Our relationship with Him is first.
- If we are married, our relationship with our spouse is second.

- If we are parents, our relationship with our children is third.
- Our work comes fourth.

So many of us have this thing backward. We spend way too much time at the office and not enough time with our spouse. Someone else spends time with the kids, and we give God our leftover time, which is very, very little. What I can tell you for sure is this: God is calling us, His children, to get it together, to discern the times. Our priorities are not lined up with His. Instead, we set up for ourselves whatever is convenient, looks good, or is a means to an end. But the best of what we could orchestrate is sorely inadequate relative to God's best for us. If we want to receive all that He has for us, we must first agree with what He values most: an intimate relationship with us. God longs for us to cuddle up to Him and live in accordance with His Word.

I've got to tell you that getting from point A (out of order) to point B (in God's order) is hard—and painful! For six months I prayed this simple, yet very effective, prayer: "Lord, I want Your order for my life. I'm in need of divine balance, and I know You can do it! I want to serve You."

I had to let go of my ungodly perceptions, my self-deception, my will, and certainly my ways, and the Holy Spirit provided the help, love, and guidance I needed. Let me tell you, though, when the Holy Spirit helps, He's like a tungsten searchlight blazing in your heart. He rummages around in the recesses and caverns that are sealed up by sin. He hunts down any and all back issues of your version of *Me Magazine,* and He brings them current just so you can reread your own propaganda and realize that that's all it is—hype. You begin to see that you're not all that you've deluded yourself to be, no matter how good a person others have said you are.

Oh, but when God cleans out the cobwebs of your life, He's doing it so He can use *all* of the talents He's deposited in you and so you can bring Him glory! He's cleaning out the cobwebs so you can serve Him in spirit and in truth—authentically, faithfully, and joyfully. He will take whatever you have surrendered to Him and then give it back, cleaned up, polished up, and fit for His use.

So I encourage you to submit yourself to the Holy Spirit's surgical knife. Permit Him to shine the bright light of God's truth on your heart, soul, and mind. He will remove any cancers so you can live. He'll leave nothing untouched except what you *choose* to still hold on to.

When we recognize that we're in a season of God's spring cleaning, when we submit to His will for the duration of our testing, and when we fashion our priorities according to His order, we can confidently wait upon the Lord. He will renew our strength (see Isaiah 40:31) and prepare us to serve, which is the final step in our spiritual success.

Practical Application

Submission is not a weakness, but a spiritual strength. Think about this fact in a practical sense. Wouldn't you rather have God's best than your perception of what's best? If so, then remember surrender is a requirement, not an option.

Spiritual Truth

"For My thoughts are not your thoughts,
Nor are your ways My ways," says the LORD.
"For as the heavens are higher than the earth,
So are My ways higher than your ways,
And My thoughts than your thoughts." (Isaiah 55:8-9)

God's viewpoint is often contrary to the way we see, but it is always more accurate. So make a habit of asking God to reveal to you His perspective in any given situation.

Sixth Steps

I am convinced that, as believers, we all must undergo an ongoing process of surrender. As Paul said, "I die daily" (1 Corinthians 15:31). Whether the Lord uses challenges in your professional life, your personal life, or both (as in my friend Kelsi's experience), God's goal is to draw you closer to Him. Remember that He—not your work, not your paycheck—is your Source of life and peace. No situation can hold you hostage if you realize that God allows His people to be tested, just as He allowed the testing of Job. The following tips might help you through:

- Step outside your situation and consider it from God's perspective.
- Examine your life to see if sin is at the heart of any problem.
- Repent of that sin and move on (see Acts 3:19-20).
- Whether or not sin is the issue, look for the lesson God is trying to teach you (see Psalm 25:4-5).
- Realize that where you are is a season ordained by God and that seasons do change (see Ecclesiastes 3:1).
- Joyfully accept this season of your testing, knowing that your faithful response will lead to God's perfection in your life (see James 1:2-4).
- Surrender your will to God's will. Ask in prayer for God's goals to be accomplished in your work and in your life (see Job 22:21-28).

Journal Exercises

- On individual slips of paper, list areas in your life that you have not completely surrendered to God. Include areas in which you really don't want to hear what God has to say: for example, your finances, your family, your future. Invite God to do a complete overhaul in these areas.

- On the front of an envelope, write a dedication prayer to the Lord, indicating your desire to surrender all these areas to Him.

- Place the slips of paper in the envelope and pray the dedication prayer whenever you notice yourself slipping into old patterns.

A Daily Life of Surrender

I'm used to me, Lord.

I'm used to my ways, my likes and dislikes.

I'm used to doing things my way.

And now You come along and tell me I've got to give all
     that up?

The old me would have said,

"I don't think so."

But I see how You're working; I see how You're moving.

I understand that both of us can't lead. Lord, what are
     You doing?

I'm broken and wounded from trying to do it all my way.

So I surrender. I give up. I can't fight. I can't fuss.

Not with my boss. Not with my employees.

Not with You. Not even with my soul.

I'll sometimes have these doublespeak dialogues deep
     within myself.

"Okay, that's enough. I'm saved. God, how much more
    will You require?"
As much as it takes, I see, because You paid the ultimate
    price.
You sent Your Son, Jesus Christ, to die so that I might
    live.
And now, God, I daily just want to give—
Give back to You in what is called my profession;
My work, my labor, the life I'm confessing;
A life that is now focused on You, not just me.
It's a life of surrender found only on my knees.
When I say, "I die daily," it's because I want to live.
So help me, Father.
Help me to let go and to hold on to You.
Teach me to surrender; that's what I need to do.
In the name of Jesus I pray.
Amen.

CRISIS

Then his wife said to him, "Do you still hold fast to your integrity? Curse God and die!" But he said to her, "You speak as one of the foolish women speaks. Shall we indeed accept good from God, and shall we not accept adversity?" In all this Job did not sin with his lips.

JOB 2:9-10

Crisis can come in a variety of ways. God's Word says to not be surprised by trials. They are sure to come. It also says that, when I speak, I should "do it as one speaking the very words of God" (1 Peter 4:11, NIV). I should speak the Word. I should speak only what lines up with the Bible—when I'm in crisis just as when I'm not.

A few important observations arise from this passage from Job juxtaposed with 1 Peter 4:11. First: Someone very close to Job—his wife! —challenged him to speak against God. Second: Job's integrity was on the line. Would he speak godly words or not? Third: Job endured his crisis by accepting the good as well as the bad in his life's circumstances. Fourth: He took great care with the words that emerged from his mouth. And he did not sin with his lips.

Lord, please help me guard my heart against those who may tempt me to sin, especially those who are close to me. Lord, please help me maintain my integrity when I go through various trials. Lord, please help me to accept all of what You allow to come my way, the bad as well as the good. Moreover, Lord, please guard my mouth so that I might not sin against You.

Action Point: Today I surrender my desires—for justice, for explanation, for quick remedy—to Your grander intentions. I especially surrender my words, asking You to guide my tongue.

INSTRUCTION

The law of the Lord is perfect, reviving the soul. The statutes of the Lord are trustworthy, making wise the simple. The precepts of the Lord are right, giving joy to the heart. The commands of the Lord are radiant, giving light to the eyes. The fear of the Lord is pure, enduring forever. The ordinances of the Lord are sure and altogether righteous.... By them is your servant warned; in keeping them there is great reward.

PSALM 19:7-9,11, NIV

When I get dressed in the morning, ready for the day's journey, let me remember to also "put on the Lord Jesus Christ" (see Romans 13:14). When I set my mind on glorifying God, our enemy will be displeased. One of the best ways for him to get me off track and off task is to throw obstacles in my path. Instead of experiencing God's best, he desires me to be encumbered by daily worries in the workplace; his every effort will be focused on getting me to "take off" the Lord Jesus Christ so that my flesh will have opportunity to "fulfill its lusts."

The first way in which I can fight back, equipped with the full armor of God (see Ephesians 6:10-13), is to surrender my will to God's instructions, as the psalmist said.

My faithful obedience will allow the power of His might to work on my behalf. Lord, I have decided to "walk properly" before You, knowing that, by my righteous surrender to Your instructions, You will equip me to conquer the devil.

Action Point: Today I seek God's instruction before going into battle.

CHAOS

For where envy and self-seeking exist, confusion and every evil thing are there. But the wisdom that is from above is first pure, then peaceable, gentle, willing to yield, full of mercy and good fruits, without partiality and without hypocrisy.

JAMES 3:16-17

Lord Jesus, give me wisdom from above. It's not easy to embrace the wisdom found on the job. I'm surrounded by people with different degrees, opinions, and agendas. Every day I encounter people who have lots of book knowledge, but not necessarily any spiritual discernment. If I'm not prayerful, I'll be sucked into their chaos and fall victim to their confusion. But I am careful to ask You to give me the wisdom of heaven. Imbue me with power from the Holy Spirit.

Lord, let the words from James 3 be a daily warning to me. I choose now to resist the spirit of envy. I reject any self-seeking interests that lead to confusion, which Your Word calls evil. Instead, I want wisdom that is pure and peaceable, gentle and willing to yield. Help me, Father God, to be full of mercy and to bear only good fruit that brings You glory. Help me to walk at work without partiality. Lord, let my yes be yes, and my no be no, so hypocrisy won't follow me. I want to avoid chaos and lay hold of righteousness, for when I do, You will bring peace. For You, dear Lord, will order my steps and direct my path (see Proverbs 3:6) this day and every day. Teach me, God, to be a wise peacemaker.

Action Point: Today I dodge chaos by prayerfully believing God will supply the wisdom I need (see James 1:5).

DETOURS

As he journeyed he came near Damascus, and suddenly a light
shone around him from heaven. Then he fell to the ground, and
heard a voice saying to him, "Saul, Saul, why are you persecuting
Me?" And he said, "Who are You, Lord?" Then the Lord said, "I
am Jesus, whom you are persecuting. It is hard for you to kick
against the goads." So he, trembling and astonished, said, "Lord,
what do You want me to do?" Then the Lord said to him, "Arise
and go into the city, and you will be told what you must do."

ACTS 9:3-6

Father, in the name of Jesus, I pray that this day You will direct me on any detour according to Your will. With a deep breath and a big gulp, I give You permission to take me down a road I never thought I would go. I ask that You speak to me from heaven and reveal to me who You are and how I might be persecuting You even now. If I am doing anything that undermines my walk or the walk of others, open my blind eyes so that I might see the error of my ways. When I am prepared to chase after You with a heart and mind to do Your will in this place, I will prayerfully await Your instructions, Lord. I trust You will tell me what I must do.

Father, it is with great anticipation that I listen for Your direction because I know that when You set me on the path of Your choosing, I will finally be heading down the right road. Today, even though I may find myself on an unexpected course, I will open my eyes to the reality that, no matter what, I am on it by Your divine will.

Action Point: Today as I encounter the unexpected, I ask the Lord for His direction and protection.

HOLINESS

The parched ground shall become a pool, and the thirsty land springs of water; in the habitation of jackals, where each lay, there shall be grass with reeds and rushes. A highway shall be there, and a road, and it shall be called the Highway of Holiness. The unclean shall not pass over it, but it shall be for others. Whoever walks the road, although a fool, shall not go astray.

ISAIAH 35:7-8

I want to walk on that road where, even if I falter by making bad or foolish choices, I shall not go astray. When my professional ground is parched, God's Word says it "shall become a pool." When I find myself thirsty and in need of divine protection, God's Word says I will find "springs of water" even in hostile territory. In order for me to get on that road, however, my walk with Christ must live up to its name: Highway of Holiness.

The holiness road will lead to success in all that I do. And what does it mean to be holy? It means I set myself apart from the world, consecrating my life for God's purposes. It means I cut sin out of my life so that I can be clean. Holiness must be mixed into every aspect of my daily life. Holiness will allow all that I do to prosper in due season.

What a comfort to know that God will guide and protect me even when I make mistakes! It would be ideal if I could perform at my best level every day of the workweek, but the reality is I can't. However, His "strength is made perfect in [my] weakness" (2 Corinthians 12:9). When I find myself the fool, I ask the Holy Spirit to teach me, and I continue down the Highway of Holiness.

Action Point: Today I ask God to reveal any sin in my life that keeps me from the way of holiness. I pray for the strength to overcome.

ANXIETY

Be anxious for nothing, but in everything by prayer and supplication, with thanksgiving, let your requests be made known to God; and the peace of God, which surpasses all understanding, will guard your hearts and minds through Christ Jesus.

PHILIPPIANS 4:6-7

Father, could it really be that simple? Can I be free from anxiety by giving You all my concerns? Your Word tells me to be anxious for nothing, but this job has me on edge more often than not. Be they deadlines or delays, politics or positioning, my worries keep coming one after the other, like waves on the shore. I don't want to find myself overtaken by the incoming tide.

Today I purpose in my heart to not let anything or anyone steal my joy. You have promised to work *all things* together for my good (see Romans 8:28). What a magnificent invitation You have extended to me, to give You all my anxieties in prayer! Thank You for taking them from me.

Lord, I give You my fear. Lord, I give You my faults. Lord, I give You my frailties. Lord, I give You my future. I accept in return a heart and mind guarded by Your Son, Christ Jesus.

Action Point: Today I make the decision to live in a state of prayer, thanksgiving, and peace, knowing that when I come to You, heavenly Father, with all my apprehensions and all my fears, You will meet my needs and give me peace.

PRIDE

Pride goes before destruction, and a haughty spirit before a fall.
Better to be of a humble spirit with the lowly, than to divide the
spoil with the proud.

PROVERBS 16:18-19

A simple check of the headlines proves that, far too many times, pride causes those in power to fall from grace. Their greed, covetousness, and cavalier attitudes are evidence of their lack of integrity and love for others. Rather than point at the faults of others, may each public exposure prompt me to check my own heart for pride. Have I completely surrendered my sin of pride to God and asked Him to replace my will with His? I must do this regularly.

Lord, I pray that any pride in me will disintegrate and that Your love in me will be strengthened. I pray You will never let me fall victim to that spirit of pride that ensnares so easily, especially when You are showering Your blessings upon me (see Deuteronomy 6:10-15)! A word of warning goes a long way for those with a teachable spirit. Father, please keep my spirit receptive to Your reproof. Knowing that pride goes before destruction, I reject any prideful notions that allow me to think more highly of myself than I should (see Romans 12:3). Knowing that a haughty spirit goes before a fall, I ask You, O God, to shower me with the blessing of humility.

Action Point: Today I prayerfully examine my heart for signs of pride and ask God for wisdom about how to permanently lay them aside.

SILENCE

To everything there is a season, a time for every purpose under heaven.... A time to keep silence, and a time to speak.

ECCLESIASTES 3:1,7

I am committed to doing good because God delights in my desire to please Him. So today I decide to quietly go about my daily tasks. In the quiet of my mind, I will whisper prayers of thanksgiving as I do my work. My heart will sing praises to the Lord for His goodness and generosity. I will listen for the sounds of silence in my inner soul, because I know God has placed me right here, in this job, "for such a time as this" (Esther 4:14, KJV).

My silence is not idle because I can translate every thought into a prayer for those around me, releasing the mighty power of God who answers the prayers of His people. I know there will be times when I am called to cry out to Him on behalf of those with whom I work (see Hebrews 5:6-8). People are in need of direction, comfort, love, and acceptance.

Help me, Father, to support those around me by extending my prayers and not always my words. Revealing Christ's love through the excellence of my work, I silently wait on You, Lord, and on Your purposes to be revealed. Father, help me to respect everyone I work with and let Your love be exemplified through my actions toward all people, especially toward those here on the job.

Action Point: Today I silently rejoice at the wonderful work that can be accomplished through prayer, quiet support, and the whispers of Christ's love.

WISDOM

Happy is the man who finds wisdom, and the man who gains understanding; for her proceeds are better than the profits of silver, and her gain than fine gold.

PROVERBS 3:13-14

Father, I want to joyfully embrace all You've given me to do. I want to profit from a deep understanding of Your desires for me. I want to be a person who finds wisdom and, therefore, happiness in my work.

Daily, I will strive to gain a greater appreciation of Your will and Your ways. I believe all You have promised about wisdom in the "wisdom book" of Proverbs, including this: "When you walk, your steps will not be hindered, and when you run, you will not stumble. Take firm hold of instruction, do not let go; keep her, for she is your life" (4:12-13).

May I take *firm* hold of Your instruction and wisdom. Teach me how to use those gifts as life-sustaining tools so that I might prosper and grow. Lord, help me detach myself from the false wisdom of the world and completely attach my mind to You. When I am tempted to look outside Your Word for direction, remind me to look to You. When I am on the verge of taking advice from someone who seems to know what he or she is talking about, remind me to evaluate the advice in the light of Your Word. When I have exhausted the resources provided me in order to do my job well, may I come to the knowledge that You are my greatest resource. You can make me rich with the wisdom of God if only I ask (see James 1:5).

Action Point: Lord, I glorify You this day by offering this profession of my faith: "To God our Savior, who alone is wise, be glory and majesty, dominion and power, both now and forever. Amen" (Jude 25).

INFINITE CAPACITY

Honor the LORD with your possessions, and with the firstfruits of all your increase; so your barns will be filled with plenty, and your vats will overflow with new wine.

PROVERBS 3:9-10

I am so thankful that I serve a God whose love knows no measure, whose love is limitless. Only He can promise that my barns will be filled with plenty and my vats will overflow.

This provision is based, however, on the condition of my obedience. Lord, help me to obey. You have blessed me with employment, and I know it is You who has provided for me over the years. In return, You have asked this of me: that I honor You with my possessions and with the firstfruits of all my increase. You instructed Your people in Malachi 3:10 to "'bring all the tithes into the storehouse, that there may be food in My house, and try Me now in this,' says the LORD of hosts, 'if I will not open for you the windows of heaven and pour out for you such blessing that there will not be room enough to receive it.'"

Lord, the economics of the world would tell me that I can't afford to tithe off my income. Nevertheless, I believe that when I do, You will be true to Your Word. So I open my heart and my wallet in great expectation of all You have for me. I choose to surrender my own sense of lack and be filled up with Your inexhaustible supply. I commit to the building of Your kingdom by giving my tithe either to a church or a Bible-teaching ministry that is clearly producing "good fruit" (Luke 6:43-44). Your economy has no capacity. Your love toward me is endless.

Action Point: Today I commit or recommit to God my love, my walk, my work, my gifts, and my income.

YIELDING

Woe to him who strives with his Maker! Let the potsherd strive with the potsherds of the earth. Shall the clay say to him who forms it, "What are you making?" Or shall your handiwork say, "He has no hands"? Woe to him who says to his father, "What are you begetting?" Or to the woman, "What have you brought forth?"

ISAIAH 45:9-10

Yielding to Christ in all things is one of the hardest aspects of my walk at work. I want to be in the stream of God's will for my life, going with His flow, yet when the water gets a little choppy, when the river of demands gets a little too rough, I have a tendency to say, "God, what are You doing? What are You making? What else do You want to do in my life?"

Forgive me, Father, when I challenge You with these questions. By the power of Your Holy Spirit, please gently remind me that You are the Creator who shaped the earth, which was void and without form before Your voice brought it shape and life. You are the Maker who called light out of total darkness. And just as You spoke since before eternity, "Let there be…" I know daily You speak those same three words to me, calling forth Your perfect will in my life.

Rather than withdraw from You or fight with You, Father, help me to yield to Your work in my life. I understand that You are my Maker. You are refining me day by day into a wonderful creation You can use right now, right in this place.

Action Point: Today I ask God to use me to help another person see that the work of His hands is fruitful because of what He daily is doing in me.

Tolerance

So when you, a mere man, pass judgment on them and yet do the same things, do you think you will escape God's judgment? Or do you show contempt for the riches of his kindness, tolerance and patience, not realizing that God's kindness leads you toward repentance?

ROMANS 2:3-4, NIV

Today's workplace is filled with judgmental people. It brims with employees who pretend they are upright and yet, when no one is watching, do the very same things they profess to abhor. These are the same people who pass judgment on me. "In fact, everyone who wants to live a godly life in Christ Jesus will be persecuted, while evil men and impostors will go from bad to worse, deceiving and being deceived" (2 Timothy 3:12-13, NIV). Better to endure their judgment than to share their hypocrisy!

Holy Spirit, lead to repentance those who say one thing but do another. I thank You, O Lord, for Your kindness and patience as I walk imperfectly with You. Lord, may Your compassionate tolerance lead me daily to repentance. I will pay close attention to what I must do in order "to contend earnestly for the faith" (Jude 3). I pray for the grace I need in order to persevere moment by moment in my walk of faith.

Father, I surrender to Your Word and humble myself under it for Your glory and my good. "You, however, know all about...the persecutions I endured. Yet the Lord rescued me from all of them" (2 Timothy 3:10-11, NIV). Father God, I thank You for Your never-ending tolerance toward me. Help me to live a more loving and righteous life before others, but mostly before You.

Action Point: Today I guard my lips against speaking judgments on my brothers and sisters.

THE WALK

For we are His workmanship, created in Christ Jesus for good works, which God prepared beforehand that we should walk in them.

EPHESIANS 2:10

"I am fearfully and wonderfully made" (Psalm 139:14). He holds the stars of heaven in place (see Genesis 1:16-17). Heaven is His throne, and the earth is His footstool (see Isaiah 66:1).

He causes my heart to beat, a baby to smile, the deer to run, and the mockingbird to sing. Therefore He ought not be mocked! He made me for good works, and I want to walk in a way that is pleasing in His sight.

So, Lord, empower me today to make the most of every moment. Let every word I speak and every prayer I pray honor You, Sweet Jesus, my Lord and Savior. Let me walk in the good works, Father, that You set before me daily.

Father, today let my walk at work lead others to say, "There's something special about that one. There's a light that shines from within." May others see my "work of faith, labor of love, and patience of hope in our Lord Jesus Christ," and say, "Amen" (1 Thessalonians 1:3).

Action Point: Today I ask the Lord to show me what good works He wants me to do, and then I walk in them.

CONFIDENCE

Now this is the confidence that we have in Him, that if we ask anything according to His will, He hears us. And if we know that He hears us, whatever we ask, we know that we have the petitions that we have asked of Him.

1 JOHN 5:14-15

At work people are expected to have confidence in their ability not only to get the job done, but to do it well. As a result, most workplaces are filled with enough false bravado to make the stomach churn in yet another "Maalox moment."

What exactly is true confidence, Lord? Is it self-assurance or sanctified assurance? I suspect that my confidence is not so much in my ability, but in *Christ's ability* to take His yielded vessels and wow even the most cynical of skeptics. It is because of Christ that I have the right stuff. It is because of Christ that I have what it takes to rise to the top. The key is in that word *yielded*—yielded to His will for my life, cleaned up, consecrated, set apart for His use, and familiar with His will. I set myself apart by making sure I don't have "God on my lips but the devil on my hips." I want Jesus to incline His ear to my prayers.

So, when I pray for a particular outcome at work, my confidence comes from a bold belief that God will answer my prayers when I live in a manner pleasing to Him. And while not everything I do will glorify Him, I will ask God to please lead me to try. I have confidence that He will search my heart and make me new, daily working to make me pure.

Action Point: I place my confidence and trust in the certainty that God is moving me today to turn to Him in every way. It's a wonderful thing to trust that He is with me step by step.

GLORY

Whatever you do, do all to the glory of God.

1 CORINTHIANS 10:31

Everything God does in my life will always be for His glory and my good. That is a promise and a principle I can firmly stand upon. Even when I'm going through the frustrating, painful, or seemingly pointless motions of the workplace, I know God is pushing me to rely ever more on Him. He wants to increase my faith in Him. He also wants to do a miraculous work in my life so that others will want to know the God whom I serve and so that still others will have greater faith and be led into a deeper relationship with Christ.

Since I know that God is always working for my good, my daily goal should be to do all things to the glory of Him who loves me. For Jesus said I am to abide in His love and keep His commandments (see John 15:10). Therefore:

- When I work, I should walk as a child of light (see Ephesians 5:8), working with such integrity that it will bring glory and not shame to the name of Jesus Christ.
- When I speak, I should speak words that edify others and bring grace to those who would listen (see Ephesians 4:29).
- When I walk, I should walk in such a way that others will know I am an authentic follower of Christ (see Matthew 5:16).

Action Point: Today I invite God to shine His glory through me so that others will be attracted to His light.

LOVE OF MONEY

Take heed and beware of covetousness, for one's life does not consist in the abundance of the things he possesses.

LUKE 12:15

The problem with money lies not so much in having it, but in that the love of it can get me into trouble. "For the love of money is a root of all kinds of evil, for which some have strayed from the faith in their greediness, and pierced themselves through with many sorrows" (1 Timothy 6:10).

Sometimes I look at my paycheck and wonder, *Where does all the money go?* Some goes to bills, some to expenses, and some to things I want but perhaps don't need. When I'm honest with myself about money, I must also be clear about my longing for it. I need money; everyone does. I have obligations and responsibilities, but many times I use my money in a way that does not necessarily honor God. I might purchase an item I could really do without. Do I truly need yet another pair of shoes? Do I really have to have that suit that's on sale? When does enough become too much? Enough is too much when my love for a material possession comes between my love for the Lord's kingdom and my willingness to give to God's storehouse (see Malachi 3:10). The Word calls that covetousness.

Lord, if I have strayed from the faith in any way because of greed or the love of money, speak to my heart right now so I can return to the path of righteousness.

Action Point: Today I counter my flesh's desire to acquire by giving some of my money away for the work of God's kingdom.

NEED

*For your heavenly Father knows that you need all these things. But
seek first the kingdom of God and His righteousness, and all these
things shall be added to you.*

MATTHEW 6:32-33

When I think about money and what God asks me to do with mine, I
must remember that He does not need me, but rather that I need Him.
In Psalm 50:12, He says, "If I were hungry, I would not tell you; for the
world is Mine, and all its fullness."

So if God doesn't need my money, then why do I hear all this talk
about tithing among believers? Ten percent seems like a lot of money to
me when I'm having a hard enough time paying my bills. But what if,
starting this Sunday, I tithe just as an act of obedience? What if I give 10
percent of my paycheck to help with all God wants to accomplish on
the earth? What if I just take God at His Word?

Condition: God wants my firstfruits, which means giving 10 percent of my income right off the top—not my leftovers. Believers are
called to "honor the LORD with all your possessions, and with the *firstfruits* of all your increase" (Proverbs 3:9, emphasis added). Provision:
My house will be filled with plenty! God even says to test Him on this
and see "if I will not open for you the windows of heaven and pour out
for you such blessing that there will not be room enough to receive it"
(Malachi 3:10).

Action Point: Today I become a doer of the Word, not just a hearer,
and I commit to tithe faithfully, knowing that, when I do, "my God
shall supply all [my] need according to His riches in glory by Christ
Jesus" (Philippians 4:19).

OWNERSHIP

*The earth is the LORD's, and all its fullness, the world and those
who dwell therein.*

PSALM 24:1

All I have belongs to the Lord! *My* name may be on the paycheck, on
the bank account, or on the title deed, but God's Word is clear: The
earth is His and *all* that's in it.

So today I rededicate all that I have to You. I offer it upon the altar
of my life—giving You myself, my house, my money, my life. The only
reason I have anything at all is because of Your grace, Your mercy, and
Your love. I will strive to remember that You are the Lord my God "who
gives [me] power to get wealth" (Deuteronomy 8:18).

So when I'm tempted to say, "I acquired this or that," I'll remember
that it was You all along who blessed me from on high. You have given
me charge over all that I have. Help me be wise. Help me open up the
deep well of my heart so I can offer help to someone else today. Teach
me, Father, to share the many gifts You've bestowed on me. I want to be
a blessing to my colleagues.

Action Point: Today I give thanks to You for my material blessings,
and I share with an unsuspecting coworker some of what You've given me.

PROTECTION

But let all who take refuge in you be glad; let them ever sing for joy. Spread your protection over them, that those who love your name may rejoice in you. For surely, O LORD, you bless the righteous; you surround them with your favor as with a shield.

PSALM 5:11-12, NIV

What a secure feeling, knowing that I have a constant shield of protection around me! What a comfort it is! When danger takes aim—perhaps even fires—I know that nothing could ever penetrate Your force field.

Like a spotlight, the Lord's hand of protection follows me. His eyes dart to and fro, eagerly searching to assist me. In You I will hide, Lord, underneath Your wings of love. Just the mention of Your name allows me to thrive.

If I stand in the shadow of Your protection, I can rest in Your rich affection. A towering shield, You remain the Perfecter and Protector of my faith. Your love remains a forceful constant, always at the ready. I rejoice in You and count it an honor to be divinely protected by the Word implanted in me!

Action Point: Today I seek protection in a verse of Scripture that resonates in my "right-now circumstance." Then I demonstrate my faith boldly, knowing that doing so gives glory to God.

Purpose

The Spirit of the LORD is upon Me, because He has anointed Me to preach the gospel to the poor. He has sent Me to heal the brokenhearted, to proclaim liberty to the captives and recovery of sight to the blind.

LUKE 4:18

When Jesus stood up in the synagogue of Nazareth, His hometown, He spoke simply and directly:

- He said He came with the Spirit of the Lord upon Him. Lord, I pray that the Spirit of the Lord comes upon me when I go to work today.
- He said He had been anointed "to preach the gospel to the poor." Lord, anoint me at my job so that I will see those who are poor in spirit and then gently but confidently tell them about the gospel of Jesus Christ.
- He said He was sent "to heal the brokenhearted." Lord, send me with a kind word, a loving touch, and a prayer for someone today whose heart is broken.
- He said He came "to proclaim liberty to the captives." Lord, I know that only You deliver. Give me words of life that will help someone seek deliverance from You.
- He said He came to proclaim "recovery of sight to the blind." Lord, someone today has no idea who Your Son is or why He came for him or her. Use me to open up this person's eyes to see the love of Christ and believe!

Action Point: Today I surrender and submit my will to the Lord's purposes. Lord, use me in any way You see fit today.

SERVE with All Your Heart

*And whoever of you desires to be first shall be slave of all. For even
the Son of Man did not come to be served, but to serve, and to give
His life a ransom for many.*

Mark 10:44-45

Don't you love it when you go to a dinner party or reception and
the first question someone asks is "What do you do for a living?"
Today, when people ask me what I do, I tell them I'm in the service
industry. That response either stops them in their tracks or prompts a
discussion that allows me to slip in a word about Christ. My most satisfying conversations are those that permit me a chance to talk about the
goodness of the Lord. Similarly, my most satisfying work is accomplished when I am able to serve another by pointing the way to God.

The deeper you grow in your relationship with Jesus Christ, the
more you want to serve Him and others in whatever job you're in, wherever He places you. I have left the television industry twice now, each
time prepared to do whatever the Lord asked. I just never thought He'd
ask me to go back on the air.

Six months after I left CNN, God "showed up and showed out" like
never before. I am now hosting the most spiritually satisfying television
program I have ever worked on. *America at Worship* airs every Sunday
morning and profiles various Christian worship experiences across the
United States. Best of all, I get to lift up the name of the Most High
God. Through the love He has for me and the love I have for Him, I

have the privilege of influencing viewers toward a relationship with the living Son of God, Jesus Christ.

You see, most of us think our focus at work should be gaining professional fulfillment, money, or status. That, of course, is how the world would have us view things, but God wants us to embrace a different paradigm. Whether you are the president of the United States or a janitor, you are in God's service industry if you are a Christian. Whatever your job description, your *spiritual* vocation is really all about service. When God is at the center of our lives, all we want to do is honor Him in our work.

Serving in Samaria

> For this is good and acceptable in the sight of God our Savior,
> who desires all men to be saved and to come to the knowledge
> of the truth. (1 Timothy 2:3-4)

Do you realize God wants all—even the boss and the most sluggard employee—to come to a saving knowledge of Him? If we submit to Him, God will use us believers as instruments to draw others into relationship with Him. Although the thought of sharing Jesus with those we work with can make us nervous and uncomfortable, we do better to think of witnessing as an exciting journey. A person who comes to Christ has a life-changing experience. What a joy and privilege to be part of any opportunity the Lord gives us to show someone the Way!

During the course of our lives, we are likely to spend more time working than engaging in any other activity, so let's figure out how to enjoy our *real* on-the-job assignment. Remember that Jesus sent us into the world to witness (see Matthew 28:18-20 and Acts 1:8).

In the introduction I talked about Samaria as a metaphor for the workplace (see Acts 1:8). As the leading edge of the Baby Boomers moved into their fifties, many in our culture, disappointed by the promises of worldly success, began to seek fulfillment in "spirituality." Of course not all roads lead to Jesus Christ, and we who know this have to speak up on the job and elsewhere. Jesus is who He says He is, and we are His witnesses to point others to the true Way (see John 14:6). We know that spiritual fulfillment comes *only* from a relationship with Christ.

Jesus often ministered at the workplace. Matthew was a despised tax collector. In his day, a tax collector was not exactly an exalted and worthy profession. If I had to choose a term that might accurately describe Matthew, it would be *social outcast*. If anybody needed a Savior at work, he did. You can read how Matthew came to know Christ in Matthew 9:9. Where did Jesus meet this man? He went to Matthew's workplace. How effective was Jesus in ministering to Matthew? He simply said to the tax collector, "Follow Me." At that very moment, Matthew stood up and became a disciple.

Well, Jesus *is* Jesus. So it's no surprise that he had this effect, but remember He also says to us, in John 14:11-13, we will do even greater works than these. After Jesus ascended into heaven, His disciples went into the world two by two to share the gospel. Christ sent them out together so that their lives would be examples of God's truth. We can benefit today by following the guidelines below and obeying Jesus' command that, as His followers, we share the gospel:

- Honor the fact that our walk with Him is a 24/7 commitment.
- Avoid compartmentalizing our faith.
- Show our love for Christ by loving others (see Matthew 25:31-40 and John 21:15-17).

God calls believers into active service. When we obey, we are covered by the incredible prayers of Christ in John 17 and the priceless intercession of the Holy Spirit (see Romans 8:26-27). The unease (dare

I say "dis-ease," or "disease"?) we have about sharing the Truth has caused many of us to be guarded. But what is truth except that which agrees with reality? We have to get past being guarded and start taking pride in our calling as witnesses for Christ.

Serving Up Real Solutions

> There are different kinds of gifts, but the same Spirit. There are
> different kinds of service, but the same Lord. There are different
> kinds of working, but the same God works all of them in all
> men. Now to each one the manifestation of the Spirit is given
> for the common good. (1 Corinthians 12:4-7, NIV)

Offering Christ or Christian work ethics to a coworker is no doubt a real service. Sometimes simply presenting colleagues with Scriptural principles as a solution to everyday problems is all that is needed to open the door to their hearts, especially when they act on those principles and achieve positive results!

Remember my friend Ed from chapter 4? Frustrated by a difficult relationship with a difficult supervisor, Ed was ready to throw up his hands. I told him to, instead of giving up, fall down on his knees and petition God on his boss's behalf. Ed did that. Now he and his supervisor have experienced a complete turnaround. Almost daily, Ed finds himself in a situation where God can use Him further to introduce Christ to his boss and his colleagues.

Don't worry about forcing open the door of opportunity. The Holy Spirit will arrange the right moment for you to witness. And *witness* is a loaded word, isn't it? Know, though, that our testimony is not only what we confess from our mouths, but is also evidenced by our walk at work. When we establish our presence as a Christian and earn credibility as someone who is consistent and reliable, then we can speak Christ into almost any situation. This is really the most important form of service we can perform.

We don't have to wiggle or wince when the normally touchy subject of religion comes up in the cafeteria. We don't have to feel uncomfortable. After all, God is our CEO, we stand boldly on His Word, and we press on daily to be fully submitted to Him. We speak with compassion, not judgment or condescension, and we are willing to do as the song says: "Let it shine, let it shine, let it shine!" It really is true: When we shine for Christ and not for ourselves, others will be attracted to the Light. God designed our testimony to work that way, so that people can see that there's something different about us.

A Short Guide to a Happy Task

> Let your light so shine before men, that they may see your good
> works and glorify your Father in heaven. (Matthew 5:16)

With Jesus as our example, we can never go wrong in our witnessing. Prayerfully approaching every opportunity to share the gospel will yield the best results. Asking the Holy Spirit to give us the necessary discernment, sensitivity, and words means there will be more of Him and less of us, and that's always a good thing!

- *Initiate relationships.* Oftentimes Jesus was the one to spark a conversation. We can seek opportunities to grow our relationships at work by simply speaking to others first. (See Mark 5:25-34; John 4:7-42; and John 5:1-16.)
- *Maintain a good reputation.* Jesus approached people right where there were, and many times that place was where they worked. His reputation oftentimes preceded Him, and these

people sought Him out! His good works were evident through His good deeds. (See Matthew 4:21-22 and John 4:7-42).

- *Speak Christ into the situation.* Jesus spoke to others of what He saw the Father do (see John 8:38). Let us do what Jesus did. Pointing others to the Truth, to who Jesus is, will give them hope, joy, and eternal life. Ask them questions about their spiritual journey, just as Jesus asked people (see John 8:1-11). Telling others about Christ doesn't always have to be some "heavy" conversation. It can simply be about what He has done in your life (see Revelation 12:11).

- *Look for opportunities to serve.* Jesus said that those of us who want to be the greatest must become the least and that those who want to be served must serve others (see Luke 9:48).

- *Move from pondering to praying.* Because we are commanded, "In everything by prayer and supplication, with thanksgiving [to] let [our] requests be made known to God" (Philippians 4:6), decide that in crisis, confusion, or conflict you will stop thinking and start praying.

- *Decide, no matter what, to count it all joy.* "My brethren, count it all joy when you fall into various trials, knowing that the testing of your faith produces patience" (James 1:2-3). Even in the midst of deadlines and deals, choose to be joyful. Whether you are constantly pulled or finally promoted, remember that patience is perfected by joyfully enduring.

If God is so gracious to use us to bring others to repentance and into relationship with His loving Son, Jesus Christ, let us joyfully serve!

Practical Application

> Thus says the LORD: "Let My people go, that they may
> serve Me." (Exodus 8:20)

The only demand Moses made of Pharaoh over and over again was that he let God's people go so that they may serve Him. God wants us to serve Him in our walk and in our work. As a matter of practicality, let's begin to realize we don't merely work to serve man or even ourselves. It is God's design that we would serve Him with gladness.

Spiritual Truth

> If anyone serves Me, him My Father will honor.
> (John 12:26)

It is truly a gift to devote the work of our hands to God's glory and to share the love of Christ with our coworkers. When we do so, God bestows honor upon us and invites us to enter into His joy.

Seventh Steps

- Ask God to give you opportunities at work to initiate relationships and conversations with people who don't yet know Him.
- Study the Word faithfully. As you practice this discipline, the Holy Spirit will remind you of the right things to say, and you will become better equipped to speak Christ into any situation at any time.

Journal Exercises

For one week, before you get to work, ask the Holy Spirit to reveal to you over the course of the day three opportunities to serve God. Write about your experiences each evening. At the end of the week, see how many times you were given opportunities to pray for others, encourage others, admonish others, or simply bring the joy and good news of the gospel to others. Spend time praising God for the privilege of serving Him.

In Silence I Serve

Day by day, in silence I serve. I work not just for pay,
But for all He deserves.
Lord, continue to show me, continue to lead me.
Help me exalt You in thought, word, and deed.
As I head through the doors in this place where I work,
I put on the full armor of God like a shirt.
It says, in Ephesians 6:13-18, if I am to stand
I must put it on and hold only to Your hand.
Right now I speak and put on the belt of Truth,
Now girded about my waist,
The breastplate of righteousness also firmly in place.
My feet are shod with the gospel of peace,
My faith shield, Christ paid for;
It's not just on lease.
The helmet of salvation is firmly on my head.
The sword of the Spirit defends all that You've said.
I will continue to watch as well as to pray.

I will steadfastly serve in silence—day by day.

What an honor to be on assignment in the service
    of the King.

It is a privilege to which I daily will cling.

Thank You, God, for calling me into service for You.

In Jesus' name I pray this prayer of truth.

Amen.

ATTITUDE

Your attitude should be the same as that of Christ Jesus.

PHILIPPIANS 2:5, NIV

If I am ever going to come close to having the attitude of Christ who humbled himself (see Philippians 2:8), I've got a lot more work ahead. Today I will work on my attitude. Today I will also remember that "I can do all things through Christ who strengthens me" (Philippians 4:13).

I admit that some days are easier than others, but when I approach my work with an attitude of thanksgiving and service, the day goes more smoothly. My work is more productive, and people naturally gravitate toward the life of Christ in me. Therefore, in my heart right now, I've decided to adopt a daily attitude that permits my light to shine. "The people who sat in darkness have seen a great light, and upon those who sat in the region and shadow of death Light has dawned" (Matthew 4:16).

Whenever I yield myself to the Holy Spirit for His use, I can do so joyfully. I want my attitude to reflect the fruit of the Spirit. Lord, on this day help me to extend love, joy, peace, longsuffering, kindness, goodness, faithfulness, gentleness, and self-control to my boss, my coworkers, my subordinates, and my superiors (see Galatians 5:22-23).

Action Point: Today I resolve to keep my attitude in check, even if people persistently push my buttons, knowing that I may be the only light they will ever see pointing the way to God.

ABUNDANCE

So let each one give as he purposes in his heart, not grudgingly or of necessity; for God loves a cheerful giver. And God is able to make all grace abound toward you, that you, always having all sufficiency in all things, may have an abundance for every good work.

2 CORINTHIANS 9:7-8

God loves a cheerful giver! When I joyfully give from my heart, I not only bless the recipient, but I receive blessings as well. I become the object of God's love. He offers me grace and gives it abundantly to me for every good work.

Lord, on this day, may I do good works at my job. May I cheerfully extend a helping hand. May I joyfully perform the tasks ahead. Your Word says You love a cheerful giver, so I give graciously and happily from my heart. Even when I get tired, even when frustration looms, may I remember Your love and realize I want that more than anything.

Father, I know I will never lose by giving, so help me go the extra mile, patiently pursuing the task at hand. If I offer up a smile, a kind word, or even a small gift to someone who needs it, I am the winner because the gift is in the giving. What does it cost me to bring some joy into my office? Nothing. What does it mean to me if I remember to bring it? Everything. For Your love is everything to me.

Action Point: Today I happily and abundantly pour from my heart and give my time and my talents.

DOER

But he who looks into the perfect law of liberty and continues in it,
and is not a forgetful hearer but a doer of the work, this one will
be blessed in what he does.

JAMES 1:25

The law of the Lord is perfect, and that law gives me liberty. When I consistently seek to do God's will, then I have freedom that no one can ever take away. I don't have to be a slave to the fickle winds of change in my work environment. I don't have to bow down to individuals who need attitude adjustments on a daily basis. I just have to stay the course, not forgetting that my assignment is to live and work as the Holy Spirit guides.

When *I* am a diligent doer of God's work, and if I do not forget what He tells me in His Word, I will be blessed in all that I do. Lord, this day, by the power of Your Holy Spirit, bring to my remembrance those words that have fed my spirit. Holy Spirit, speak clearly to me so that I might hear You and follow Your lead. Sweet Jesus, whisper into the ear of the Father on my behalf and ask that He bless the work of my hands.

Action Point: Today I put into action one principle I have learned from chapter 7 about serving others, and I walk the walk at work.

HONESTY

*That you also aspire to lead a quiet life, to mind your own business,
and to work with your own hands, as we commanded you, that
you may walk properly toward those who are outside, and that you
may lack nothing.*

1 THESSALONIANS 4:11-12

Honesty is one of those attributes that people tend to view in relative
terms. "He's fairly honest." "You can generally trust her." How sad is
that, when we have to measure on a curve something that should be
pass/fail?

God's Word is black or white. I'm either honest—or I'm not.

Lord, I want to be an honest person, an honest worker, and an honest friend, but I know I'm going to need the Holy Spirit's help. He will
teach me how to be truthful in all things (see John 16:13).

Do I work in a way that is beyond reproach? Or are there certain
aspects of my attitude and actions on the job that I would rather not
have under a microscope? Here's a daily truth checkup:

- Have I uttered any word that was not completely honest?
- Have I used the resources of my employer for personal gain
  without asking permission?
- Have I accounted for all my time on the job, working as
  unto the Lord?

Action Point: Today I carefully examine every aspect of my behavior
and speech, testing each for truth—not relative truth, but God's ab-
solute truth.

"I Am"

Then Moses said to God, "Indeed, when I come to the children of Israel and say to them, 'The God of your fathers has sent me to you,' and they say to me, 'What is His name?' what shall I say to them?"

And God said to Moses, "I AM WHO I AM." And He said, "Thus you shall say to the children of Israel, 'I AM has sent me to you.'"

EXODUS 3:13-14

I want to walk so closely to God that when I speak to others they can know that I AM has sent me. Just like Elohim (see devotional in chapter 1), I AM is a name that defies description. That's because God Himself cannot be confined into one word or one meaning. He encompasses too much for that.

When I focus on I AM, He can use me to lead others into a deeper and more meaningful walk with Him. When Moses set out for Egypt to ask Pharaoh to free the children of Israel, it was for one reason and one reason alone. God said, "Let My people go, that they may serve Me" (Exodus 8:1).

God's intent is no different for me today than it was for the Hebrew people. I need to let go of anything that holds me back from serving God, whether that be money, power, addiction, lust, or laziness. I want to be free from all things that keep God from using me. I want to be able to say to those I serve, "I am here because I AM sent me."

Action Point: Today I keep my eyes on God so that He can use me to serve others and meet their needs.

JUDGMENT

Judge not, that you be not judged.... And why do you look at the speck in your brother's eye, but do not consider the plank in your own eye?

MATTHEW 7:1,3

This judgment thing really is a balancing act, and I want to get it right. On one hand, God admonishes us not to judge another or even to judge anything before its time because that judgment is God's job. He will expose the motives of a man's heart (see 1 Corinthians 4:5). On the other hand, as a believer called to exercise spiritual discernment, I am to judge "all things" (1 Corinthians 2:15) So exactly what does it mean to judge righteously on a daily basis as I continue my walk with Christ?

The Holy Spirit will help me see the truth of any situation. The Holy Spirit will reveal to me where people are coming from and whether they have good or bad intentions. The Holy Spirit will let me know if I'm out of line when examining somebody else's issues without first looking at my own (see John 16:8,13).

Holy Spirit, help me to stop pointing my finger without paying attention to the three pointing back at me. Rather than judge others for where they are and what I think they should be doing, let me instead look to You for guidance to determine how I should respond, with a word or perhaps a prayer. I leave it to You to handle the shortcomings of others; my only job is to keep my heart in tune with You. Teach me how to lift Your children up in prayer rather than tear them down with my words or in my mind.

Action Point: Today I rein in my temptation to judge another person and instead pray for both of us.

LAZINESS

Because of laziness the building decays, and through idleness of hands the house leaks.

ECCLESIASTES 10:18

I have my lazy days just like everyone else. While resting is good—even commanded by God—there is a difference between rest and idleness.

Some people have perfected the popular practice of "vegging out." Their work ethic is different on weekends or in the evenings, maybe because their supervisors are a rare sighting. They have convinced themselves that after hours no one is really watching them or evaluating the quality of their work. But God is watching. He sees the manner in which I work every moment of every day, for He peers into my heart and thoughts (see Matthew 9:4).

Others have a low regard for people who don't pull their weight, and according to God's Word, laziness causes decay and idleness. Even the lowly ant has figured out that if you don't work, you don't eat (see Proverbs 6:6-8). Similarly, God expects me to do the work of bringing in a harvest for Jesus. He commands me to "walk worthy of the Lord, fully pleasing Him, being fruitful in every good work" (Colossians 1:10).

Whether I am home and need to attend to repairs or at work where my job requires me to go the extra mile, working as unto the Lord makes laziness take a backseat. Deciding to work hard becomes medicine for an idle mind, and productivity results.

Action Point: Today, as I'm tired and totally beat, not wanting to work yet knowing I must eat, I remember that laziness will bring decay to the purposes God has for me.

MINISTERING

Who then is Paul, and who is Apollos, but ministers through whom you believed, as the Lord gave to each one? I planted, Apollos watered, but God gave the increase.

1 CORINTHIANS 3:5-6

At times I speak with passion and conviction about my beliefs, but the people I'm talking to are either not ready to hear what I have to say, uninterested, or slightly offended, feeling I've come on just a bit too strong. They ask, "Are you a minister?" And I reply, "Hey, I'm just a believer."

Well, the truth is we're all ministers. Not all of us have theology degrees or ordination papers, but because of our commitment to Christ, He commands us to share the gospel. And what does *gospel* mean? The word translates as "good news" (Mark 16:15, NLT).

But it's so important for me to remember that, apart from God, I will be ineffective in ministering with His message of hope, especially in the work environment. My *sensibilities* tell me to be aware of certain religious *sensitivities*. Rather than coming on like gangbusters, I just need to do what God asks of me and remember that someone plants, someone else waters, but it is God who gives the increase.

Rather than feeling bad because the reception on the other end was ho-hum at best, I rejoice in the fact that I've been obedient to Father, and I trust that He'll take care of the rest. Sharing the good news is worth the risk because there will be those around me who will come to believe because I opened my mouth. That's not just a good thing; it's a God thing!

Action Point: Today I won't be discouraged by my ministry efforts even if they backfire. Instead, I obey the Lord and trust Him to complete the work He has started (see Philippians 1:6).

MORALITY

We put no stumbling block in anyone's path, so that our ministry will not be discredited. Rather, as servants of God we commend ourselves in every way: in great endurance; in troubles, hardships and distresses; in beatings, imprisonments and riots; in hard work, sleepless nights and hunger; in purity, understanding, patience and kindness; in the Holy Spirit and in sincere love; in truthful speech and in the power of God; with weapons of righteousness.

2 CORINTHIANS 6:3-7, NIV

That's such a powerful scripture that I really need to meditate on every word. What a benchmark of morality! I wonder how I measure up on all those points. I've worked hard, and God knows He's worked in me too. Truth be known, however, I have failed and faltered so much that I wonder why God chooses to use me at all.

But I don't want just to be used by the Master; I want desperately to be approved by Him (see Matthew 25:21). I don't want to be like the believers who went to Jesus and said, "Didn't we do all these things in Your name?" And Jesus said, "Yes. But I never knew you" (see Matthew 7:22-23).

It breaks my heart to think that I could go through life believing I'm doing the work of the Lord only to discover that He was using me as a means to an end. God will accomplish His will by whatever means He sees fit. He *used* a donkey to rebuke Balaam (see 2 Peter 2:15-16).

Lord, I want to be used *and* approved by You, holy and acceptable in Your sight, which is my reasonable service to You (see Romans 12:1).

Action Point: Today I ask God to reveal what He approves in my life and what He does not, so that by His grace and power I can grow.

REJECTION

I am a reproach among all my enemies, but especially among my neighbors, and am repulsive to my acquaintances; those who see me outside flee from me.

PSALM 31:11

While it would be nice to think that everyone I come in contact with will see God's light in me and love it, Scriptures tell me something else.

Because I am a follower of Christ, who Himself is "the light of the world" (John 8:12), His light is in me. But I need to understand that just as people rejected Him, they will also reject me. Some people may actually be turned off by my countenance of joy and love. They may not understand my desire to live for Him. After all, when Jesus was hanging on the cross, even His friends stood far off, watching from a distance as He breathed His final breaths (see Luke 23:49).

At work I have more acquaintances than Christian sisters and brothers. I understand that although I may have good relationships with many of them, when I turn my back or leave to go home, some will talk about me, some will turn against me, and some will even sabotage my efforts on the job.

Their actions are painful to be sure, but it's still all good. I'd rather live for Christ than be loved by the world. I don't want to be embraced by others but rejected by my Savior. "If you are reproached for the name of Christ, blessed are you, for the Spirit of glory and of God rests upon you" (1 Peter 4:14).

Action Point: Today I won't take rejection personally. Instead, I see it as an indication that Christ's love is desperately needed where such rejection is allowed to exist.

Business Plans

Now listen, you who say, "Today or tomorrow we will go to this or that city, spend a year there, carry on business and make money." Why, you do not even know what will happen tomorrow. What is your life? You are a mist that appears for a little while and then vanishes.

James 4:13-14, NIV

As I conduct every kind of business, let me always keep God first. It is so easy to get caught up in the grind of planning and accomplishing that I forget to be about my Father's business (see Luke 2:49). Even as I make my plans, I should be mindful that God orders my steps, and He may have a different agenda for me today (see Proverbs 16:9).

Our human plans tend to obscure God's greater goals for us. He's not just about getting the account. He's certainly not just about making money. I could be so intent on meeting a deadline or making a quota that I miss an opportunity He wants me to seize for Him and His kingdom work. I don't know what might happen in the office right after I shut down the computer or turn the lights out behind me. How many times has reality changed in an instant?

Lord, enable me to see opportunities to glorify You in what I do this day. Lord, speak to my heart as I make my plans. Father, guard my mouth from boasting about what I will do. Instead, keep my mind ever stayed on You.

Action Point: Today I pray to carry out my plans in accordance with heaven's perspective.

BLESSINGS

A faithful man will abound with blessings, but he who hastens to be rich will not go unpunished.

PROVERBS 28:20

Today's headlines are filled with stories about corporate executives, businesspeople, and others who let greed motivate their business dealings. Get-rich-quick schemes fail. So do the actions of those who chase "fast money" while compromising their personal integrity and harming others.

I want to be one who abounds in God's blessings, not one who will bring shame to His name. Whenever I hear about someone's plan to gain wealth quickly, whether it is legitimate or not, may God help me walk away. May I look instead at God's desire for my financial standing, for it is "He who gives you power to get wealth" (Deuteronomy 8:18). I will be faithful over my business transactions. I will stay accountable to God for dealing truthfully with others. I will not look for a shortcut to riches, for if I do, I will likely stumble, fall, and suffer the consequences.

Lord, I will remain faithful to You and Your desires to bless me exceedingly abundantly above all that I could ever ask or think (see Ephesians 3:20). I receive true wealth when I receive what You have in store for me. I want Your blessings to overtake me because I have obeyed the voice of the Lord (see Deuteronomy 28:2).

Action Point: Today I say no to quick-money temptations, trusting the Lord to provide all I need in His perfect time.

RENEWAL

And do not be conformed to this world, but be transformed by the renewing of your mind, that you may prove what is that good and acceptable and perfect will of God.

ROMANS 12:2

Renewal is a state of mind, body, and spirit that I must maintain in order to live in the perfect will of God. Sometimes when I'm at work, my mind can get so bogged down with the do's and don'ts, musts and won'ts, that if I don't take a time-out to renew my mind, I'll find myself slipping into "an attitude."

Lord, I notice in Romans 12:1-2 that You link my body's state of holiness with my state of mind as well as my ability to live according to what is good and acceptable in Your eyes. I want to always be in the center of Your will, and if getting there means I must make sacrifices to attain purity, honesty, love, and praise, then help me, Lord, to make them. I think about the sacrifice You made for me at Calvary. How could I give You anything less than what is my "reasonable service"—a life of holiness (Romans 12:1)?

Even though circumstances at work sometimes get to me, let me not focus on the things of this world, but instead only on You. Change me, Lord; renew my mind day by day so I will always choose Your will, Your way.

Action Point: Today as I feel the patterns of the world threatening to engulf me, I take time out and ask God to renew my mind and have His Spirit lead me.

WEAKNESS

But he said to me, "My grace is sufficient for you, for my power is made perfect in weakness." Therefore I will boast all the more gladly about my weaknesses, so that Christ's power may rest on me. That is why, for Christ's sake, I delight in weaknesses, in insults, in hardships, in persecutions, in difficulties. For when I am weak, then I am strong.

2 CORINTHIANS 12:9-10, NIV

What a wonder it is to be able to delight in weakness! Lord Jesus, when I feel weak, help me get to the place where I can look past the hardship and difficulties and see nothing but Your sweet grace. Tuck deep within my heart the truth that Your Word, Your power, Your perfection are all I need.

Work can be a pretty tough place. Insults and hardships are sure to challenge me. But I thank God for Jesus, who supplies all my needs. When I am weak, He is strong. When I'm down, He lifts me up. When I'm on *E,* He fills my cup.

For Christ's sake, I will delight rather than despair in my inability to overcome trials and tribulations, for the joy of the Lord is my strength. I know He will see me through. He is my Comfort, my Rock, and it is He who renews. Truly, my weakness is made perfect in His strength.

Action Point: Today as trials come my way, I accept them joyfully because the everlasting grace of Jesus will see me through.

HONOR

He who does not backbite with his tongue, nor does evil to his neighbor, nor does he take up a reproach against his friend; in whose eyes a vile person is despised, but he honors those who fear the LORD; he who swears to his own hurt and does not change; he who does not put out his money at usury, nor does he take a bribe against the innocent. He who does these things shall never be moved.

PSALM 15:3-5

Lord, I want honor to be an integral part of my work style. May my honor for You and others be evident in my obedience to Your Word. Lord, I offer You a code of honor based on Your definition of what it should be. May it serve me well to use Your standards as my own for corporate behavior:

- I will not backbite with my tongue or speak evil against any coworker.
- I will not "take up a reproach against" another or criticize the works of his hands.
- I will dislike those things that You dislike: evil, vile, and disgraceful ways.
- I will honor people who fear You and want to please You.
- I will never take a bribe or trade favors that would be displeasing in Your sight.
- I would rather suffer to my own disadvantage than stray from the standards You have established.

Action Point: Today, Lord, may I honor You in all things, and may the work I do speak of Your glory.

MERCY

Blessed are the merciful, for they shall obtain mercy.

MATTHEW 5:7

Mercy is often viewed as an antiquated concept, but the Lord knows it shouldn't be. To show mercy means to offer kindness, to extend compassion, to be understanding and forgiving. In the workplace, mercy is needed more now than ever before. Lord, let mercy begin with me.

- When someone makes a mistake, let me remember that I make mistakes too.
- When a colleague missteps, remind me how many times I have faltered.
- When a coworker is having a rough time, let me be compassionate in my approach.
- When a supervisor is dissatisfied with my performance, let me respond with humility, not defensiveness.

Father, You said that if I am merciful to others, You will have mercy on me. What would I do without Your mercy? Without Your forgiveness, where would I be? Mercy is what You desire for me to extend to others, and I want it too. Let merciful living become such a part of who I am that my actions begin to change my work environment from within the walls of my office and through touching the hearts of my coworkers. Help my words and actions reflect my relationship with You. Help me be merciful, Father God, as an expression of You.

Action Point: Today as someone fails me or offends me, I am quick to mercifully forgive rather than reject that person or seek justice.

VACATION

My Presence will go with you, and I will give you rest.

EXODUS 33:14

One or two weeks away from the job offers a welcome break from the daily grind, but sometimes I just can't wait until my vacation begins! So whether my extended time away is in the immediate future or several months away, I take minivacations in the moments of my day and find rest in the presence of my awesome and mighty God.

Holy Spirit, before I enter my workplace, I invite You to come beside me, speak to me, guide me. In Your presence I will find rest each step of every day. May Your love surround me. Your truth and Your light warm my soul. I thank You, Lord, that I can find rest even as I toil.

Truly getting away is certainly a blessing in my life—a vacation provides me with time off, time to think, time to sit and feast upon Your Word, time to reconnect with family, time to laugh with friends, and time simply to be still.

Yet, I thank You, Lord, that I don't always need to go away to find Your perfect peace. I can steal a moment or two to be quiet in the grace of Your presence. I can listen peacefully for your Voice in a moment of divine space. Such moments water my thirsty soul, calming me and filling me. The refreshment I receive cannot be described. These secret moments of meditation are mine alone to enjoy. I know You're there, as close as my very soul, so I enter Your rest and sigh with peace.

Action Point: Today I think of my daily quiet time with the Lord as a minivacation that will reenergize me for the service Jesus calls me to do.

VIRTUE

Finally, brethren, whatever things are true, whatever things are noble, whatever things are just, whatever things are pure, whatever things are lovely, whatever things are of good report, if there is any virtue and if there is anything praiseworthy—meditate on these things.

PHILIPPIANS 4:8

Virtue is not some old-fashioned Puritan term. Neither should we regard it as a noun. Virtue is like a verb in that it needs to be put into action.

In the workplace—amid office politics, condescension, gossip, and power plays—I believe virtue still has its place. No matter how I try, I always seem to get caught up to some degree in the sticky details of the day. Not today, however. Not tomorrow or in the coming days. I will choose to resist. I will fix my mind on Jesus, on whatever is true, noble, just, and pure. I will attempt to model His goodness, His love, and His mercy.

If a statement is not true, I won't even consider it. If it's not noble or just, then I will close my ears. I will meditate on true, noble, just, and pure things today, seeking only to do God's will. I remember what I've received from the Spirit of the Lord: His peace, His joy, His truth; God's Word and His ways; God's love. I want to embrace for myself that which He deems as good. When I walk into this workplace each day, I will press on to the goal of being virtuous in Jesus Christ. Virtue is a spiritual gift from the One who alone can bless. Now, there's a promotion worthy of all my hard work!

Action Point: Today I am on the lookout for what is praiseworthy, and I devote my efforts to the pursuit of that in word as well as in deed.

PRIORITIES

So that they should seek the Lord, in the hope that they might grope for Him and find Him, though He is not far from each one of us.

ACTS 17:27

Lately life has been so hectic and crazed that time itself seems lost. Forgive me, Lord, for not slowing down enough to hear Your voice. It is in quiet times when I'm alone that You speak softly to me. What's important now is that I do not abandon this time because I cannot afford to lose it.

These past few months at work have been incredibly busy—not just work, but life and family, too. It seems that everybody around me needs something of my time, my love, my ear, my heart, or an encouraging word. Lord, You know I care about them, but I care more about my relationship with You, and lately that, too, has been suffering. You are my true priority, but making You first on my list is something I need help with, especially since my full-time office job takes up so much time. I'm tired of subsisting on popcorn prayers, so no more one-minute sessions with a quick look at Your Word.

I want to get back to the heart of who You are. I long to spend time with You, real time, when I'm not rushed to do anything but bask in Your presence. Work is important, but sometimes work just has to wait. When I start my day with You, when I take the time to simply be, I am much more productive because I bring more of You to work with me.

Action Point: Today I plan some *focused* time with the Lord.

BALANCE

Give us this day our daily bread.

MATTHEW 6:11

Maintaining balance between the personal, spiritual, and professional aspects of my life means I must feed myself with the Word of God every day. It means I must go to Him in prayer with one simple request: "Father, give me this day my daily bread."

- My daily bread is time with God.
- My daily bread is a commitment to balancing work time and prayer time. I won't let the requirements of my professional life devour my intimate time with the Lord—even if I must get up early to spend time with God before heading off to work.
- My daily bread is the inner joy I express toward God and others at work.
- My daily bread is love in the midst of the day's tension. It is the indescribable and awesome love I know Jesus Christ has for me. Lord, let that love emanate to all those around me today and every day as I partake of You.

This daily bread brings renewal. So, today at work, I am going to find a prayer closet in which I can talk to God and cry out to Him and go to Him for refreshment. He sustains and fills me with the ultimate "power lunch."

Action Point: Today I derive my spiritual energy from the Bread of Life by taking time out of my day to feast on God's Word.

The True Measure of Success

*Give, and it will be given to you. A good measure, pressed down,
shaken together and running over, will be poured into your lap.
For with the measure you use, it will be measured to you.*

LUKE 6:38, NIV

I f a man is measured by his own mind, he will revert to self-deception
and illusions of grandeur. (You know that "he's a legend in his own
mind" routine.) If we rely on ourselves as barometers of our success,
we'll believe we've achieved something great, when, in reality, we may
have failed miserably. The truth is that apart from God we are nothing.
With Him, we can do all things through Christ who strengthens us (see
Philippians 4:13). It is critical, therefore, if we want to really succeed,
that we gauge our progress according to God's Holy Word. It is imperative that Jesus be our only Standard.

If we want to *experience true success* on the job, in our homes, or
wherever else the Lord might lead, we must live our lives with an ever-
increasing faith that won't fail in the face of trial. We must permit the
Holy Spirit to build our faith according to both where we've been and
how the Lord has brought us through. As He consistently "shows up
and shows out" in the midnight hours of our lives, each moment of triumph can be a building block on which we add more blocks of belief.

If we want to *enjoy meaningful success,* we must practice prayer on a
regular basis, prayer that is ever maturing. At some point when we were
young, we moved from, "Now I lay me down to sleep" to conversations

with God based on the promises in His Word. Our prayers should move from self-centered prayers designed to bless us to selfless prayers presented to God on behalf of others.

If we are to *reflect success* at work, we must triumph daily by staying close to our Source. When we are challenged—go to the Word. When we face difficulties—go to the Son. When our hearts ache—cry out to the Father and believe that He will hear from heaven. For it is our Father's good pleasure to give us the kingdom.

Our primary commitment to God in all things brings us right back around to where we first started. Let us *seek first* His kingdom and His righteousness. Let us be about our Father's business, no matter where He has placed us. This is His command, and this is His purest desire for us apart from salvation.

> And do not seek what you should eat or what you should drink, nor have an anxious mind. For all these things the nations of the world seek after, and your Father knows that you need these things. But seek the kingdom of God, and all these things shall be added to you. Do not fear, little flock, for it is your Father's good pleasure to give you the kingdom. Sell what you have and give alms; provide yourselves money bags which do not grow old, a treasure in the heavens that does not fail, where no thief approaches nor moth destroys. For where your treasure is, there your heart will be also. (Luke 12:29-34)

If we want to gain the treasure that only a successful life in Christ can bring, we must open our hearts and receive the Most High King. Listen for His voice, obey His commands, and be available to Him daily on demand.

Do not be afraid to ask in prayer for the power of the Holy Spirit.

Boldly use the authority that our Father in heaven has freely given to us modern-day disciples. Remember that true success on the job is ours for the taking when we choose to walk authentically for the Lord—our Creator. Seven simple steps are all that you need to live the blessed life and walk victoriously at work.

Seek Him first by...

Uniting with the Word and with other believers. May
    we daily choose to...

Change and grow to be more like Jesus...

Committing ourselves afresh to God's plan and purposes
    for our lives, while...

Enjoying our walk at work...

Surrendering to, and...

Serving the One True Living God...and His name
    is Jesus!

I pray that you will celebrate true S.U.C.C.E.S.S.
    in Him all the days of your lives.

In Jesus name.

Amen.

Index of Devotionals

STEP 5: ENJOY

STEP 6: SURRENDER

About the Author

©Kristen Feller

A ndria Hall is coauthor of *This Far by Faith: How to Put God First in Everyday Living* as well as president of SpeakEasy M.E.D.I.A., Inc., a media and public-presentation consulting firm offering media coaching, broadcast quality productions, and public speaking services. She presents *The Walk at Work* as a movement, an authentic and viable way of living one's vocation (www.TheWalkatWork.com).

The author conducts Walk@Work workshops and other faith empowering seminars. She is a professional inspirational speaker whose dynamic down-to-earth message is blended with humanity and humor, insight and a gentle insistence that we must embrace God, honor our spirit, and practice the grace of Jesus Christ as we follow the path to success.

Andria currently hosts a Faith and Values Media, Sunday morning program called *America at Worship*. The program is available to some fifty million homes and airs weekly on The Hallmark Channel. Previously, Andria served as weekend anchor with CNN/USA for two years. Her affiliation with this breaking-news leader placed her in one of the most visible roles in global television news. She is "successfully" married and the mother of three.

For more information about SpeakEasy M.E.D.I.A. or Andria Hall, log on to her Web site at www.AndriaHall.com.